Puff

Puff

A true story of love, hard work, patriotism, achievement, and an uncompromising spirit; intertwined with war, greed, violence, and criminal justice

by Paul Devantier

Chaumiére Communications
Arbor Vitae, Wisconsin

Copyright © 2013 Devantier LLC

All rights reserved. No part of this book may be reproduced or transmitted in any form or by means, electronic or mechanical, or by any information storage and retrieval system, without written permission from the author, except for the inclusion of brief quotations in a review or article related to the book.

Published by Chaumiére Communications, Arbor Vitae, Wisconsin. Chaumiére Communications is a division of Devantier LLC.
2509 Schuman Road, Arbor Vitae, WI 54568
chaumierecommunications@gmail.com

ISBN: 978-0-9888938-9-4

Book design by Patricia Bickner

Printed in the United States of America

Dedicated to all those who have engaged in public service and have demonstrated a strong commitment to family, country, integrity and a diligent work ethic.

INTRODUCTION

P*uff* is the story of a man, and the principles and people he loved. It is about the risks he took, the things he pursued, and the compromises he would not make.

In a sense, it is about a generation and a time that is swiftly fading from the memory and consciousness of those born in the second half of the twentieth century. Heinz Puff is not "every man," but those with whom he grew up and those who helped define life for him shared common experiences that shaped their lives, too. He experienced immigration to the United States. He was just a little tyke in the Roaring Twenties. He grew toward manhood in the Great Depression Thirties, and experienced firsthand the World War II Forties.

Not unlike others of his generation, Heinz Puff discovered that life was not always easy. Some in every generation claim their right as victims and simply resign themselves to a life devoid of experiences and achievements they fantasize would bring more joy.

Others find ways to look past the challenging realities to make things work. They are just too stubborn to give up or admit they are not capable of fashioning their own destinies. Puff is a champion of this group of people. In fact, this book is an insightful tribute to all that is wholesome about stubbornness—and, perhaps, a few less than wholesome things.

When given the choice to knuckle under to situations and circumstances that were not right or fair, Heinz resisted. When given just a limited number of options, Heinz expanded the number. When the latest fad in society swept through, he watched from a distance, not easily drawn in. When his concept of what was truly right and proper was challenged, he stood his ground.

For some, inflexible attitudes and behaviors are not to be applauded. Even with Heinz, as he would admit, there are times when a little compromise would make sense. And there are times when standing firm for things of little consequence probably doesn't make a lot of sense. Still, Heinz turned many of his stubborn attitudes and behaviors into virtues that served his family, friends, and country well. But in doing so he suffered a fair share of sacrifice and loss.

Puff is about hard work, love, sacrifice, forgiveness, and achievement despite the odds. It is about an uncompromising spirit, a commitment to integrity,

Introduction

and a disarming sense of humor. *Puff* is about twists and contradictions, too—war, separation, greed, homicide, criminal justice, and personal loss.

Puff is a true story.

I
THE WAR AND BEFORE

"You, soldier, wake up! Look at me. What are you doing here?" It was the not-so-pleasant voice of the Sergeant.

"Sir, I don't know exactly," was the reply.

"Do you know *why* you are here?"

The young man looked around and couldn't answer the question. He, too, wondered why he was on a bed in the sick tent. "No, sir, I don't know why I am here."

So the Sergeant explained. "I understand that you and Corporal Puff and a few of your friends went off to one of our neighboring pubs last night. And I'm told you and the others drank the place dry of brandy and whiskey. Someone was nice enough to bring you here after you passed out. The headache you are feeling has nothing to do with being in a war. It's just a reminder of your own stupidity. Now get up, there is work to do."

And the soldier responded as quickly and coherently as he could. "Yes, *s-s-sir!*"

It was Australia—a country that would become a relatively short stopping-off point for troops from the United States. The ultimate mission put the troops in much more dangerous and painful situations—much more so than the pain brought on by a hangover. But at this point the soldiers, who may have never traveled more than fifty miles from home, were just seeing things and places they had never even expected to see, enjoying some new-found friends, and "having a good time" whenever possible. They had not yet experienced war with all its varied and unending unseemliness.

The year was 1942, shortly after the bombing of Pearl Harbor by the Japanese. Since its entry into World War II, the United States military was waging war on many fronts. The battles in the Pacific that began with Pearl Harbor were expanding. The Japanese army had a stronghold in the Pacific in the area that included New Guinea and the Philippine Islands. There was some disagreement among those directing the U. S. war effort concerning the engagement of the Japanese in these areas, but it was apparent that a serious threat existed that needed to be addressed. American troops were stationed in a number of places in the Pacific.

Some 11,000 troops of the 32nd Division were serving in the Pacific. The division consisted of National Guard Units from Wisconsin and Michigan. It was not at full strength, since it did not have all the

The War and Before

equipment it required. Included in the division was the 126th Field Artillery Regiment of the Wisconsin National Guard. Among those serving in Battery A of this regiment was a young man named Heinz G. Puff.

Heinz had never experienced jungles. The weather, terrain, and warfare way of life were as distant from his Milwaukee, Wisconsin, way of life as was the geographical separation. The cold winters of Wisconsin were nearly vanished memories in the heat of the jungle. Weighing in at 151 pounds upon entering the military, he left the Philippines at the end of his 39-month tenure overseas at less than 140 pounds.

Heinz and his colleagues faced the ambitious task of defeating the Japanese and securing strategic areas for use by U. S. armed forces in the Pacific theater. Heinz was assigned what he later called "one of the easy jobs." Actually, there was nothing easy about it, but it *was* a small step removed from the front lines.

Heinz was responsible for transporting, setting, and manning machine guns and large howitzers. He and his fellow soldiers assigned to this detail would move into a contested area and make the first move on an enemy target or stronghold. Having established their presence and cleared the way, soldiers would proceed to engage the enemy. There were many times that the resistance from Japanese combatants would put Heinz directly in the line of fire.

Occasionally, in the process of entering a new area in New Guinea and later in the Philippines, Heinz and those around him would encounter ambushes. But as Heinz would say, "By the grace of God I was spared." Heinz would go on to say, "In a sense, that bequeaths a responsibility. You have an obligation to do something meaningful, to live with integrity, to show that the life that was spared is a productive and contributing one." The army experience was one of the factors—a very strong one—that helped shape the rest of Heinz's life.

The army buddies surrounding Heinz came from a variety of places, but most were from the upper Midwest. On quieter nights and between periods of open fire, they would talk. There were several in particular that Heinz came to know, appreciate, and respect.

One was an Italian whose parents immigrated to the United States. Their customs and traditions were different, yet in many ways similar to those Heinz knew. Roots are important to most people. Heinz saw roots as important, but not what determines how one faces life. The "now" was more important than the "then." His Italian friend felt the same way. The differences were not something that got in the way of

The War and Before

their friendship, although they did from time to time argue about whose heritage produced the best food. Given the involvement of both Germany and Italy in the European theatre of World War II, homeland was a subject that frequently surfaced.

Another was the son of a fairly wealthy businessman in Milwaukee. His life had been simpler in many respects than the one Heinz had lived. And he seemed a whole lot more timid than Heinz. Being a soldier scared him considerably. But he took a liking to Heinz as one whose emotions were well under control. And Heinz looked out for him, knowing what a difficult ordeal the war was for him.

Apart from conversations about the war, battle tactics, and next day strategies, talk of back home was common.

"So, I heard you were born in Germany, Bud." (For reasons Heinz cannot fully explain, his nickname in the army was Bud.)

"Yeah, but I don't remember much about it. I was pretty little when I came with my mother and my brother, Gerhard, to America."

"And now you are part of a war against Germany. If you had not come to America, you could be fighting on the other side."

"I don't think too much about that."

It was true. Heinz certainly knew of his German

roots, but nearly all of what he had experienced in life was in the United States. "America is my country," he proudly proclaimed. "It is the only one I have known. In fact, I have only a few slight memories of my time on earth before coming to America. I don't really remember Germany, and at this point in my life I have no real desire to go there. Maybe someday when the war is over. Maybe."

There were other fellow soldiers who had come to the United States from Germany and elsewhere. Most, however, were born in the States. On the few and far between quiet nights, they would share stories of their own childhoods and stories they had heard from their parents and other family members.

Though not one to be especially verbose as the young soldier that he was, Heinz would occasionally chime in. "I don't even remember getting on the ship to come to America, but I do have a few lingering memories of being on the ship. And there are only a few things I remember from Germany."

"Isn't the weather in Germany a lot like that in Wisconsin?" someone asked.

"I think it is," said Heinz, "and I do remember being in snow as a little kid. We were in Dresden where I lived and my father was going to make a short trip to the butcher shop. There was a lot of snow on the ground. So he put me on a sled and took me along.

He was pulling the sled, but there was a slight hill we went down getting to the butcher shop. I guess the sled picked up a little speed on its own and I tumbled off. I can still see my father laughing and laughing. Guess it must have been pretty funny. Then, when we got to the butcher shop, I remember getting a small piece of sausage from the butcher."

"Is that why you still like sausage so much, Bud?"

"Maybe . . . or maybe it's just in my German blood or maybe I'm thinking about it because we don't seem to get a lot of good sausage here in the jungle."

"Oh—and one other memory from those days—an early embarrassing moment, you might call it. I think we were visiting my grandmother and grandfather for some party that my grandmother was having. So my mother had me all dressed up, handsome little kid that I was—as you can surely imagine, looking at me now. And my mother let me go outside to play. My brother, Gerhard, and some of his buddies came along, and I followed them down to a nearby river. I don't think it was a really big river – maybe just a good-sized creek. You guys can probably see what is coming. I slipped and fell and ended up in the muddy water. There was no threat of drowning. The water wasn't very deep, but now I was soaking wet and my nice clothes were not so nice looking.

"It was a long trip back to grandmother's house. I

don't know if I was simply scared or embarrassed or what, but walking into the house was not a pleasant chore. So there I am, still dripping, and I remember my grandmother stripping me of those nice clothes, standing me on the kitchen table bare-assed, drying me off, and looking for other clothes that I could wear. It's funny what you remember, isn't it?"

Heinz didn't think a lot about Germany being his boyhood home. By this time in his life he was fully committed to *his* country, the United States. Still, he couldn't help but think about family members he had never met or couldn't remember who were still in Germany. He does recall that later in the war, when Dresden was so devastated by bombing, he did feel a small part of himself wounded as well. Also, he remembered well the stories his father told of being in the German army in World War I. One generation fighting for Germany, and the next generation fighting against it.

Heinz could have told stories about conflicts in his own family, in addition to conflicts between nations. But some things were not necessarily things one would discuss with fellow soldiers. Heinz loved his father and his mother and always credited them with providing for him a good life. He was especially close to his father throughout his father's life, even though, as Heinz would say, "apparently I was a bastard." He didn't know until after his father's death that he was born before his father and mother were married.

He did know that his brother, Gerhard, was his father's child by another woman —his aunt, his mother's sister. Gerhard was older than Heinz and he was raised by Heinz's father and mother, not by his birth mother. He was part of the family when Heinz came along, and as far as Heinz could remember, there was never an issue about Gerhard's origin. The Puff family was perfectly typical of most families Heinz knew in Milwaukee. He remembered the tough years of the Great Depression in the 1930s, during which he was a pre-teen. What he experienced was similar to what so many others were experiencing, but his father always had a job and the family managed to survive and to make plans for the future.

"We ate a lot of soup in those days," he recalled. "I would go to the grocery store with my mother. Meat was often 'too expensive,' she would say, but she always managed to get some bones from the butcher for making soup."

Though initially engaged in New Guinea, Heinz and his comrades eventually ended up in the Philippines. The early days in actual combat situations remained a blur of sorts for Heinz. There was a lot of movement. There were a lot of changes in command; a seemingly never-ending change in assignments. What

Heinz does remember is the swampy conditions often encountered—the insects, the diseases contracted by fellow soldiers, the non-stop cascade of perspiration in the jungles of New Guinea. The 32nd Division was among the very first to experience real combat in World War II. Heinz's infantry group, the 126th, was initially partnered with Australian soldiers in the first assaults on positions in New Guinea.

There were days when things seemed relatively quiet, and other days when his division came "face-to-face" with the enemy. Heinz frequently was sent on patrol to determine if there was any movement toward them by the Japanese troops. Heinz also participated in setting out booby traps around the encampment of his unit. The goal was to keep the troops as safe as possible, knowing full well that safety in a war zone was an important but unattainable goal.

Despite the best attempts of Heinz and his fellow soldiers to have clear warning of the enemy's proximity and movements, one tragic incident showed how difficult that assignment was. One morning at the first light of day, two men who were serving as cooks for the unit were found dead in the camp where Heinz's unit was. Their throats were slashed. It was apparent that the attack on these men had happened during the night while the soldiers slept, and that the enemy had entered the camp without being detected by those on guard duty, or by any of the men in the unit. Even though the Japanese soldiers had not been seen, it was an encounter that was as close to a face-to-face meeting as any encounter could be.

On another occasion, on routine patrol in an area where it was thought there were no enemy soldiers, a hand grenade exploded very close to where Heinz and his comrades were. It was another example of how close the Japanese soldiers could get to the Americans without being detected. Over a period of a month or so, an old airplane made occasional visits, flying at a low altitude over the American encampments. There was no indication that the pilot or plane posed a serious threat. In fact, the visits became an amusement to the soldiers, who dubbed the pilot "Washing Machine Charlie."

As time went on in the various war venues, friendships grew. One soldier Heinz considered a close friend was named Tommy. What brought the two together was their love for fishing. Wisconsin was a great fishing state. Growing up, Heinz and Gerhard and their father would go fishing frequently. Heinz knew a lot about freshwater fish. He didn't know a lot about saltwater fish, but his friend did. Tommy had spent some time in Florida and told tales about deep-sea fishing. Heinz would talk about the thirty to forty-pound muskies in Wisconsin lakes. Tommy would talk about the hundred-pound saltwater fish off the coast of Florida. The two even made plans to go into business after the war. They would buy a boat in Florida and, for a fee that would eventually earn them a good living, they would take people fishing. What a great way to go, they thought. Doing what they loved to do and making some money in the process. They actually talked quite a bit about the dream, refining and revising their plans as the war days in the jungles dragged on.

The only time Heinz had experienced saltwater was on his way to America. It was another rare glimpse into his early childhood, and he would tell the story on numerous occasions. His father was already in America, so he traveled with his mother and brother.

"I remember my mother and my brother, Gerhard, getting quite seasick. I remember ending up in the ship's dining room alone. I can't imagine such a young kid being allowed to wander around the ship alone, but I guess there wasn't much chance of a kid running away or being kidnapped.

"At any rate, here I am in this dining room. There weren't many people, but there was another young kid. So the waiter sat us down at a table. I guess I didn't know what to order . . . or maybe I was just smart enough at that tender age to know the nice man would bring us something good to eat.

The War and Before

Heinz Puff as a young child. This photo was taken shortly before he boarded a ship with his mother and brother to travel to America.

"Well, that was my introduction to ice cream. Had never had it before. Maybe that's why I still remember the incident."

Heinz was four years old at the time. In fact, he turned four while he was on the ship coming to America. "I don't remember my birthday on the ship. My mother told me later that I turned four while we were at sea. But I do remember the ice cream. Oh, and there's one other thing I remember very distinctly. I was standing by the railing with my brother Gerhard when a lady's hat blew off her head. The wind must have been pretty strong that day. We watched the hat carried by the wind make its way down to the water. And as we watched the hat floating up and down amidst the waves, we saw a dolphin or two playing with it."

Since all immigrants from Europe had to enter the United States through Ellis Island, that is where Heinz and his family were introduced to their new country. In addition to being the entry point where immigration papers were checked and verified, immigrants were subjected to medical exams to check for infectious diseases and other conditions that could be a burden on people already living in the United States.

In 1926, when the Puffs arrived, Ellis Island had been the federal immigration entry point for more than 30 years. In the earlier years of the twentieth century, some one million immigrants a year entered the United States through Ellis Island. The numbers diminished significantly during World War I. For a time, it was a holding place for German merchant ship crews and others thought to pose a threat to the United States. During the first World War, Ellis Island was also used as a place to provide some initial medical services to sick and wounded soldiers returning from the war.

With new quota regulations enacted by the United States government, the numbers of immigrants passing through Ellis Island were around 125,000 a

The War and Before

year in the mid-1920s when Heinz, his mother, and his brother, Gerhard, arrived.

Heinz's recollection of the experience was another of the few retained memories from his early childhood. "I was separated from my mother and brother and found myself in an examining room. Everyone was examined physically—to avoid health problems coming into America, I suppose. Anyway, there I was—a bare-assed little boy on a table, with strangers looking me over."

"Say, Bud," said one of the soldiers, "that's the second bare-assed story you've told us. You must have a great memory of the times others saw you in your birthday suit."

"Well, it doesn't bother me now," said Heinz. "That's the way I sleep. All the time. Too hot here for wearing clothes to bed in this part of the world!" Interestingly, that practice of his in New Guinea and the Philippines became a life-long habit, even in the much colder climate of Wisconsin.

Heinz doesn't remember how he and his mother and brother got from Ellis Island to Milwaukee. They knew all along that Milwaukee was their destination. Heinz's father was already there and had secured a place for them to live. It was a small, two-family house on 25th Street, on the near north side of Milwaukee, complete with an outhouse in the backyard. The sole heat source for the house was provided by a wood-burning stove in the kitchen. There was no running water.

After a short time in this residence, the Puff family moved up in the world to a larger, two-family house in the same neighborhood. This one had running water and indoor plumbing. Heinz recalls how impressed he was that it even had a water heater. His father would have to go down to the basement to light the water heater, but it was so much nicer than having to heat water on that wood stove.

The Elm Street school that Heinz attended was just a few blocks away. Classes were taught in English, although most of the students and many of the teachers in this largely immigrant community spoke German. "I got in a few fights over the language," Heinz admitted. "I was happy to learn English, and I knew quite a bit of it by the time I started school, but since so many of the people were able to speak German, I wondered why we couldn't just speak German once in a while. It didn't seem right to expect a rather total abandonment of one's native tongue.

"I remember one teacher who was not German and was very insistent when it came to language. I was not her favorite pupil. She had a large glassed-in display case in her classroom filled with stuffed birds. When someone was 'naughty' in the class, she made them stand for a period of time in front of the display—looking at it and away from the rest of the class. By the time I moved on from her classroom, I could name every single bird in that cage —in English, of course."

From early on, Heinz was not given to compromise in areas where compromise meant giving up something of significance. He respected authority, but was never pleased when authority was abused. He understood the value of legitimate rules and always sought to obey them, but he did make his own feelings known when he believed the rules were not fair or did not accomplish what they were intended to accomplish.

"There has to be a better way," Heinz would say many times. More often than not, the better way Heinz envisioned had to do with the way people were treated. He could never countenance dishonesty or arrogance or the desire on the part of some to ascribe to people different classes, with some higher and more privileged than others. He believed from early on what his new country had taught him: that all people are created equal and that they are "endowed by their creator with certain unalienable rights" including "life, liberty, and the pursuit of happiness."

Most of the people Heinz knew or knew about in Milwaukee felt the same way. There were many immigrants in Milwaukee. They congregated in enclaves within the city of Milwaukee. There were people from Germany, Italy, Croatia, Poland, Hungary and so forth. They retained a part of their background and heritage, while interacting with others who had similar backgrounds. They kept traditions such as native cuisine alive. Milwaukee had a vast variety of excellent ethnic restaurants. Still, despite holding on to some of their roots, most immigrants considered themselves Americans. They all pledged allegiance to the flag of the United States and they were happy to be citizens. Although it took a while, they all worked hard to learn the English language.

While Milwaukee came to be known as a strong German city, it was not always easy for Germans in Milwaukee. During World War I, Germans were among the least popular citizens. Many recent immigrants to Milwaukee from Germany were still loyal to Kaiser Wilhelm II of Germany. Some had relatives fighting for Germany. When the United States, in 1916, adopted a position in opposition to Germany, Germans became somewhat suspect. After the United States entered the war in 1917, dislike and suspicion of Germans intensified. For the rest of the war years and well into the 1920s, being German in Milwaukee was anything but a societal plus. In fact, some Germans even changed their names to avoid being easily identified as German.

The War and Before

Fortunately, the blatant anti-German sentiment dissipated as the years went by. The 1920s became a time of frivolity and pursuit of the good times, and disdain based on ethnic identity waned. A new national policy emerged in mid-1919 that shifted the attention of many U. S. citizens away from the war and ethnic hostilities—prohibition.

At this time, the production of beer was not a critical industry in the city, but beer was identified with Milwaukee and Milwaukee with beer. In fact, Carrie Nation, who led the temperance movement, claimed that if there was any place that was "hell on earth," it was Milwaukee. One of the reasons for such hyperbole may have been the fact that Milwaukee not only produced beer, but had a super-abundance of neighborhood bars—an average of about one for every 230 residents.

When Heinz arrived in Milwaukee as a youngster, the intense feelings about Germans were becoming less of a public issue. Milwaukee and all of the country were moving quickly toward the 1929 event that would change life for all those living in the United States—the stock market crash and the beginning of the Great Depression. Milwaukee's economy survived into the Depression years longer than many city economies. But by 1932, the number of those employed had been cut by more than half. Still, Milwaukee residents got through it, due in part to the strength of the ethnic groups that made up the population. People of like ethnicity stuck together and helped one another out. By the end of the 1930s, Milwaukee was doing quite well on its road to economic recovery.

In the mid-1930s, Heinz was beginning to make his transition out of boyhood. By the time he entered high school, the Puffs had moved to an even nicer flat on 24th Place. It was one of several multi-family houses owned by a couple who would become very much a part of Heinz's life after the war.

Heinz attended Boy's Tech on the south side of Milwaukee. It was quite a distance from where he lived, but walking so far was no big deal. Most children walked to school. When the weather was nice, he would ride his bicycle. Occasionally, in really bad weather, he would take the trolley.

Heinz was a soccer player. He started playing soccer at the age of eight and continued playing until he was eighteen. Numerous soccer clubs were scattered around Milwaukee at the time. The club Heinz was involved with was comprised principally of German Americans. There were Bavarian clubs and Croatian clubs and a smattering of others.

During the winter months, Heinz's club would practice in a gym attached to a larger German club where folks would gather for food, entertainment and conversation. In summer, the team would practice at a nearby field and play teams from other clubs. The disciplined practice on his team was a valuable lesson for Heinz. The effort was rewarded with championship after championship. The competitions were mostly friendly, but Heinz admits that every year some fight would break out when playing the Hungarians.

Life seemed to be quite normal. Heinz had friends and lived in the same kind of house as his friends. He was doing well in school, preparing for a career as a tool and die maker. He had a place to call home, good parents, and an older brother he liked a lot, even though he did not see too much of him. But two things happened during his high school years that would shake the stability of his world and rob him of some of his innocence.

He arrived home from school one day to find his mother announcing that they were moving—"they" meaning she and Heinz. Gerhard was already off on his own. Heinz had no inkling that his parents' marriage was coming apart. Heinz and his mother moved abruptly to another location in the city. It happened to be the house occupied by his mother's boyfriend.

Broken families were the exception in the 1930s. Today, they are more common and more accepted. For Heinz, it meant moving to a new part of town and adjusting to a new "father." All in all, Heinz adapted to this rather radical change. It was not his place to question it or to resent it. He loved his mother and respected his stepfather, but could never get very close to him. He missed his father, Arthur, a lot.

Several years passed while Heinz continued his schooling, thought about his future as a tool and die maker, and stayed in touch with Arthur. Frequently, on Friday nights, Heinz would meet his father for a movie at a theater on Green Bay Avenue. Arthur Puff had moved in with several other single men. He liked westerns, and there were plenty of good cowboy movies at that time. Heinz enjoyed the time he could spend with his father. In fact, the bond he had with Arthur seemed to grow during this time—a bond that remained strong for the remainder of his father's life.

Before Heinz graduated from Boy's Tech, his father met a woman who had been widowed. They eventually got married. Heinz was invited to move in with them, and he did so quite willingly. He was happy to be reunited with his father, and he liked the woman the elder Puff had married.

In addition to the breakup of his parents' marriage, Heinz's relatively calm childhood world was unraveling with the growing sense that his brother, Gerhard, was heading in a dangerous direction and doing things that were simply wrong.

The War and Before

By the time Heinz was a teenager, Gerhard had already been arrested for disorderly conduct and theft. He had spent some time behind bars. Heinz did not understand. What would lead his brother to engage in such destructive behavior? He thought about it a lot, but there seemed to be very little he could do. Heinz was about eight years younger than Gerhard. Given that age difference, there was not a strong and close relationship between them. Heinz looked up to his brother, but as time went on, there were fewer and fewer reasons to do so. Gerhard liked fancy, expensive cars and clothes. He liked to gamble, and he was not afraid to take something that was not his. None of these things were in any way characteristic of Heinz.

When Heinz was eighteen years old, he joined the National Guard. He was motivated not only by his willingness to be part of the military of his country, but also by his special fascination with horses. A nearby Guard unit was a horse cavalry—A Troop, 105th Cavalry—and Heinz thought being part of that would be an interesting experience. Later in life, when he told his own children about his time with a horse cavalry, they would ask, "Daddy, did you fight the Indians?"

Heinz recalls maneuvers in Milwaukee, riding a horse on a night march just north of Capital Drive by the Milwaukee River. It was a packhorse on which had been placed large machine gun packs that protruded from the back sides of the horse. The packhorse, having a mind of its own, often got a little too close to objects on the side of the road. The result was that the machine gun packs ended up knocking down a number of mailboxes that were standing close to the road. "Unfortunately," Heinz says, "it probably cost the taxpayers a few bucks to repair all those mailboxes."

On another occasion, after dismounting his horse, Sunny, during a ride, Sunny got away. They were not too far from where the horses were stabled, but Heinz just knew he was really in trouble. Besides, the stables were across the Milwaukee River and the only way back was the Capital Drive Bridge. He didn't know where the horse was going, and he was afraid to go back to the stables without the horse. Eventually, he made his way back, only to discover that Sunny was quietly and comfortably back in his stall.

The National Guard duty was part-time service that allowed Heinz to continue the five-year course of studies at Boy's Tech. However, just months before he was to complete his studies, all National Guard troops were federalized, and Heinz found himself a full-time member of the military. The 105th Horse Cavalry would become a Field Artillery unit.

France had fallen to the Germans in June 1940. In August, President Franklin D. Roosevelt ordered eighteen National Guard divisions to be activated. The 32nd Infantry Division was among them.

Heinz was officially inducted on October 15, 1940. Seven days later, he and many other young men boarded troop trains and motor convoys in Milwaukee headed for Louisiana where the guardsmen were scheduled to train at Camp Beauregard.

Early in 1941, the division moved to Camp Livingston, near Alexandria, Louisiana. In addition to all the other firsts for Heinz, he experienced a climate that was quite unlike Wisconsin, although the worst was yet to come in New Guinea and in the Philippines. Perhaps Louisiana was just part of the conditioning for the jungles. It was in Louisiana that Heinz experienced the first death of a fellow soldier—not from anything related to combat, but from the bite of a coral snake.

The year spent in Louisiana was not especially difficult for Heinz and the rest of the 32nd Division. Planning, training and preparing were part of the daily routine. The soldiers honed their strength, mental acuity, and endurance. The food was okay and the days were not unusually long.

But everyone, including Heinz, knew that they could easily face situations much more strenuous and certainly more life-threatening. There were times when the stress of thinking about what might be coming was quite real, but for most soldiers just one day at a time was top of mind. And given their age, there was a macho attitude of invincibility, not uncommon for young men in general. Somehow, they thought, they would be the ones to succeed and survive.

Following the bombing of Pearl Harbor in December, 1941, and America's declaration of war, the division moved from Louisiana to Fort Devens, in Massachusetts. The soldiers thought they would be sent from there to Europe. In fact, the plan underway was for the division to be shipped initially to Northern Ireland. Instead, on March 25, 1942, the soldiers were notified that the division would be sent to Australia to assist in the war in the Pacific, where the Japanese were making some major advances. Heinz always speculated that there may have been some fear that his division, mostly from the Midwest and populated with a lot of "krauts," would not be as effective fighting the Germans.

Heinz said, "They were afraid that we would end up playing Sheepshead with the enemy."

The 32nd Division was substantial in size. It took 13 freight trains and 25 passenger trains to transport the soldiers of the 32nd to Oakland, California. Not all trains followed the same route across the country. Heinz's train made its way to Oakland via Amarillo, Texas. This was still a time of relative ease. The training was not easy, the hours were sometimes long, but Heinz and his fellow soldiers lived in safety. Heinz even recalls that the troop train to Oakland was fun. Though it was a long trip, the train stopped regularly and one of the soldiers always managed to get off the train, find a nearby liquor store, and load up on beer.

"We stacked the beer in the bathroom on the train, and sometimes there was hardly room in the bathroom to use it for its intended purpose," recalled Heinz.

At this point in his life, Heinz could only imagine what his military service would entail. The philosophy of most of the soldiers on the train was to "keep smiling and enjoy the moment." The military had provided an opportunity to leave their home states of Wisconsin and Michigan for the first time. By the time they found themselves on this train, they had already seen the deep south and the northeast; and now they were heading west.

After a period of time in Oakland, Heinz and the others shipped out—destination: Australia. The Battle of the Coral Sea was being fought while they were at sea. It was May 1942, and the Japanese were waging powerful battles in the Pacific. Because of the Battle of the Coral Sea, the convoy of ships carrying soldiers and a huge cache of artillery changed course. A more southern route was selected.

Eventually, the convoy set in at Port Adelaide,

Australia, in the middle of May, where the soldiers remained for a short period of time. Then the weaponry, arms, and ammunition from the ocean-going vessels were loaded on trucks, and the division made its way to Brisbane, to a camp known as Camp Tamborine. Other similar supplies were loaded on ships and transported to Brisbane.

Heinz stayed on land and remembers how many times he wanted to drive his truck on the right side of the road, but was rather frequently and forcefully told: "Puff, drive on the left . . . the left—the left!" Being in this foreign country, where people drove on the "wrong" side of the road, was just one of a new round of first-time experiences for Heinz.

Heinz recalls how royally the American troops were treated by the Australians. "Just wonderful people," according to Heinz. There were nice places to go for a beer, when time and location permitted, and the food was good and reasonable. When the soldiers were able to visit a local restaurant, they could get a large breakfast for what at the time amounted to about 25 cents. Heinz does admit that he had his fill of mutton stew while in Australia.

In August, the name of Camp Tamborine was changed to Camp Cable, named for the first member of the 32nd Division who was killed in action. Corporal Gerald Cable, from Michigan, was on a ship transporting weaponry and supplies when the ship was hit with a Japanese torpedo.

By the fall of 1942, the Japanese had made major advances, controlling a large portion of the Pacific and a portion of the Asian continent. The Allies feared that Japan would attempt to invade Australia. New Guinea became a strategic area for American and Australian troops. Earlier, it was thought that the American troops in Australia would help to defend Australia.

But it was becoming clear that an American and Australian military presence was necessary at New Guinea. On September 13, 1942, General Douglas MacArthur ordered troops of the 32nd Division to New Guinea. The soldiers were to make numerous assaults upon their arrival on areas held by the Japanese. Heinz and his comrades made the initial assault, followed by deeper penetration into the area by Australian soldiers.

A number of battles took place in the subsequent two years. Heinz recalls some of the grueling marches, cutting their way through some of the most menacing jungle areas in the world. Early battles were difficult because Heinz and his fellow soldiers were in uncharted territory, both literally and figuratively. They had not experienced war before. They had not experienced the rough environment. Besides the Japanese military, diseases such as dengue fever and malaria took their toll on the fighting men. Medical attention was not always readily available.

There were victories and defeats. Surprise attacks by land, sea, and air cut into the ability of the 32nd Division. Complicating the situation were the disagreements that commanding officers had about strategy. Despite all the forces working against them, Heinz and his comrades ultimately chalked up more victories than defeats. The 32nd was the first division to be completely tested in real war situations. The Battle of Buna was especially stressful and tiring. Initially, the battle was lost. But not for good. The division rallied and finally was victorious.

Several citations were issued to recognize the success of the 32nd Division. One came in 1943 following the Buna Campaign. It acknowledged the difficult conditions overrcome by the 32nd. "Ground combat forces, operating over roadless jungle-covered mountains and swamps, demonstrated their courage and resourcefulness in closing with an enemy who took every advantage of the nearly impassable terrain." The citation concluded: "The courage, spirit, and devotion to duty of all elements of the command made possible the complete victory attained."

Following Buna was the Battle of Sanananda, and then a brief respite—some "R&R" back at Camp Cable in Australia. Late in 1943, Heinz was back

The War and Before

to the task of fighting the Japanese in New Guinea. Heinz does not recall all of the individual battles in which his unit was engaged, but there are a few areas that remain rather clear in his memory. One was the landing strip at Hollandia, where the men were able to take a brief break from the rigors of the battles along the coast of New Guinea. The battles in New Guinea had been successful. The Japanese were driven back.

Hollandia, now a place for the American soldiers to relax, had been a significant possession of the Japanese earlier in the war. A successful American assault on the landing strip took place in April 1944, giving the strip and the region surrounding it to the Americans. While the 32nd Division was not involved in the assault, its efforts in New Guinea helped clear the way for capturing an important piece of ground, and moving on from there to the Philippines.

It had been quite a struggle. The reality of victory brought some relief and a sense of pride. Still, the soldiers were aware of the cost of victory. When the opportunity to take a break at Hollandia came, it was welcomed as a time to take at least a brief recess from the war. The downtime was well-deserved.

It was here at Hollandia that Heinz and his fellow soldiers had the chance to meet a super-star—John Wayne was visiting troops in the Pacific. "I didn't quite know how to approach him or address him," said

Heinz, "but I do remember that he looked me right in the eye, and that he had a powerful handshake."

Some who were close to Wayne claimed he had a strong desire to serve in the military. He became well known as a movie star following his breakthrough movie, *Stagecoach*, in 1939. He was 34 years old at the time of Pearl Harbor and considered too old to enter the army. By the time Heinz met him he had starred in additional films and had become a household name. He was not the only Hollywood personality to be strongly supportive of the war effort, but his patriotism seemed very genuine. It was a patriotism that became very well-known later in his life. His visits to the troops provided an early glimpse of that.

"We were feeling a bit better by the time we reached Hollandia," Heinz remembers. "It was clear that progress had been made. Despite the struggles and the losses of fallen comrades, the United States army had accomplished many objectives."

In the U. S. Army Center of Military History is an account of the period, *New Guinea – The U. S. Army Campaigns of World War II*, written by Edward J. Drea that includes this passage:

> Above all, New Guinea was the story of the courage of the GI who could always be counted on to move forward against a determined foe. It was the ordinary American soldier who endured the worst deprivations

The War and Before

that the debilitating New Guinea climate could offer. It was the lowly GI who was the brains, the muscle, the blood, and the heart and soul of the great army that came of age in the Southwest Pacific Area in 1943 and 1944. In one tough fight after another, he never lost a battle to the Japanese. Those accomplishments and sacrifices are forever his and deserve to be remembered by all.

As enjoyable as the break in Hollandia was, it did not last long. A new assignment came down from headquarters that would leave New Guinea in the rearview mirror.

Regiments of the 32nd Division, Heinz's included, were sent to the Philippines, where the Japanese had earlier landed and set up bases. "We set in at Lingayen Gulf early in January, 1945. This is where the Japanese had landed earlier in their quest to take over the Philippines. Our job was to secure the Villa Verde Trail that was being held and used by the Japanese."

It took several months to achieve success, but ultimately the Villa Verde Trail came to be known as the Red Arrow Trail in recognition of the efforts of the 32nd Division—the division that was named the Red Arrow Division.

The division commander issued a general order that brought to light the successes along the Villa Verde Trail:

The 32nd Division has accomplished its mission. The enemy has been destroyed and the Villa Verde Trail secured. A passage has been forced through the Caraballo Mountains from the Central Plain to the entrance of the Cagayan Valley, thus hastening the completion of the Luzon Campaign.

After one hundred and twenty days of fierce hand to hand combat over terrain more difficult than any yet encountered in this war, the "Red Arrow" again pierced the enemy's line. You have crushed completely another of the enemy's so-called impregnable defenses, brilliantly concluding the Division's 5th campaign in the Pacific Theater.

I desire to express to every officer and enlisted man in the Division, as well as those attached, my heartfelt appreciation of the courage and determination each has shown while playing his vitally important part in this long and arduous campaign. You have outfought and destroyed a cunning and determined enemy, an enemy occupying elaborately prepared defenses on ground of his own choosing. Your victory was impressive and decisive and one of which you may well be proud.

The Red Arrow Division gained a considerable reputation during World War II, continuing a tradition established by the division in World War I. Its symbol was a vertical red arrow with a short horizontal red bar in the middle of the arrow. It signified the ability of the division to pierce the enemy line. The symbol was a holdover from World War I when the 32nd

Division in that war was the first to pierce the line of defense established by the Germans, known as the Hindenburg Line. Keeping the tradition going, the Red Arrow Division in World War II was successful in breaking through enemy lines in New Guinea and in the Philippines.

The Red Arrow Division was the first division in World War II to send an entire unit overseas. It was the first to enter into ground combat in 1942. Members of the Red Arrow division were still active in mop-up operations in the Pacific following the end of the war. This made the Red Arrow the longest-serving division in the war. It was finally deactivated in Japan on February 28, 1946. During World War II, some 600 soldiers in the 32nd Red Arrow lost their lives. A number of memorials to the Red Arrow Division remain in Wisconsin and Michigan and a number of facilities still bear its name.

After more than three years in New Guinea and the Philippines, Heinz found that war had become a way of life. It was never easy, but there were fewer firsts. Heinz had experienced nearly everything short of being seriously wounded. There were casualties, of course, and occasionally the men would look at each other and quietly ask if this would be the last time they would see each other . . . or be seen. There wasn't a lot the men did not know about one another. Some were quiet and reserved. Others could be counted upon to be part of every conversation. Some were quite religious. Others much less so. Some expressed emotions. Others held them in. Some had a positive attitude and a good sense of humor. Others found those qualities hard to come by. Some expected the worst and others never gave up.

There may have been a little bit of each in Heinz. He was not easily categorized, but all those around him knew he could be trusted and that he would always do the best he possibly could. He was a Christian—a person of faith—but he did not wear that faith on his sleeve. He never thought of life as limited to one's years on earth, but part of an extended life arranged for him and others by a God in heaven. He never felt completely alone in whatever the current pursuit may have been. While he may not have talked a lot about his very personal faith, what he did wear on his sleeve was his loyalty to his unit and his commitment to its welfare and success.

Heinz was not one to criticize his fellow soldiers or their leaders. He did respect some more than others. He was quite detail-oriented and often spent more time concentrating on the task he was assigned than engaging in idle conversation.

Still, he was not above having a little fun from time to time, enjoying a beer or two or three when it was possible to do so, and enjoying a laugh when something humorous happened in the camp or when someone told a great story. Of course, it is no surprise that conversations among soldiers frequently involved the opposite sex.

Some of the stories, of course, involved "conquests" the men had experienced. There always seem to be some who need to brag about their sexual exploits. Heinz was never sure if the stories had any basis in fact. Telling the stories, as some men his age were inclined to do, was a way to elevate their status and get some recognition. Heinz was never impressed.

Soldiers so distanced from girlfriends also often told stories involving heartache. . It was not unusual for a soldier to admit that letters from that "special gal" back home had stopped coming. It was not unusual for soldiers, reluctantly, to admit that the girls back home that they had been bragging about for a long time were now attached to a guy back home and no longer waiting for their return. For some, separation did make the heart grow fonder. For others, separation led to . . . separation.

"So tell us of your love life, Bud." Inevitably that question would be asked of Heinz, since it was a common subject of conversation among the soldiers.

"Well, nothing serious," said Heinz.

"Come on, Bud," his inquiring fellow soldiers said,

"we told you about all our girlfriends, but we haven't heard about yours."

"Some of you know that, while we were in Australia, I met a girl named Marge. Her father was an officer in the Australian army. We had a chance to spend some time together when I got a break from duty. It was a nice. I especially liked her father. What a great gentleman! But there was never anything between Marge and me. We were friends, and being with her was just a good way to spend some time.

"Besides that, I knew a few girls back home that I considered good friends, but nothing that you guys would consider a hot romance. I did take a dozen roses to a nice young woman just before we left to come over here, but it was just because it was her birthday and my dad suggested I take her some flowers."

"So, what is her name, and did you do anything with her?" they asked.

"Her name is Caroline, and no, nothing happened between us. I don't know about you guys, but I haven't been inclined to get into that sort of thing, not that I wouldn't love the chance to have a lovely young woman to be by my side. Anyway, we met when our family lived on 24th Place in Milwaukee. Her father owned the house and I got to know her then. But I was just a kid. She's a friend. I've known her for quite a few years. She *is* beautiful, and very talented, too, but

I have no plans. OK, I'll admit that I kissed her once when we were younger, in the attic of the house where we lived. That was the house owned by her father."

"Do you hear from her?"

"Ya, some of you know that I get a letter once in a while from a Caroline. And she sends me some nice little gifts, too."

"So, is she waiting for you?

"I don't know. For now, she's just a good friend."

II

TIME TO GO HOME

The war was winding down. Word was beginning to arrive that the battles in Europe and the South Pacific had been successful. A lot had changed since Heinz first set foot on the train that took him from Milwaukee to become a soldier in the Second World War. He had experienced a loss of innocence and been matured by the war. He thought about death, the one thing a 20-something normally didn't need to worry about. His fellow fishing boat owner was killed in combat in the Philippines—one of a number of his army buddies and acquaintances who would not be returning home.

Heinz and the other soldiers were wearing thin both in numbers and as individuals, physically, when word finally came, in June of 1945, that Heinz could return home. *His* mission was accomplished. After the Armistice and the end of World War II, some of his fellow soldiers in the 32nd Division were assigned to help keep the peace in the Pacific. Due for a furlough, but given the chance to return to his home in Wisconsin, Heinz chose to go home.

Eventually, he was awarded six bars for his foreign service: one for each of his six months of service abroad. He also received a Good Conduct Ribbon, the American Defense Service Ribbon, the Asiatic Pacific Theater Ribbon with three bronze battle stars, the Philippine Liberation Ribbon with two bronze battle stars, the American Defense Medal, and the Victory Medal. There were other recognitions, as well, but as the reality of going home began to permeate his thinking, the past became less and less significant.

When word came that he would be leaving the jungles, there was a celebration of sorts, but he had misgivings as well. The dream of the fishing boat in Florida had come to an abrupt end with the death of his friend. How would the old place be? What about his friends back home? What about Caroline? What about finding a job? Facing the unknowns with a sense of resolve, he said, "The sun has never failed to rise." This was a type of mantra for Heinz. He would be fine, and life would go on. There would be new opportunities, and whatever they were, he felt confident he could engage them without faltering.

The ship left on its more than two-week journey to the port at San Francisco. During the frequent quiet solitude of the cruise he recalled some of his experiences

Time to Go Home

Today, Heinz displays some of his soldier memorabilia on a wall in his house.

in the war zone. He thought about the roughly 600 families of those killed in action in the 32nd Division who would not be welcoming their beloved family members home. He thought about those who survived serious injury whose lives would be forever affected. He felt relief for himself and for his country, and prayed he would never have to experience anything like the war again. He thought about the never-ending heat and humidity—a circumstance totally foreign to what he had known in Germany and Wisconsin. Granted, Louisiana was closer in climate to New Guinea and the Philippines, but the environment of Louisiana was child's play compared to the conditions that were routine during his tour of duty in the South Pacific.

Much of what he had gone through was a blur—a lot of the same, day after day. The trees and undergrowth, trails, trenches, and insects were similar in so many of the places he served. But there were images that, no doubt, would remain. Being surprised by the enemy, and his heart beating so fast that he feared it would explode; sore muscles—lots of them; nightmares. He knew that when he got home, he would feel renewed appreciation for simple things such as a cold beer, a warm shower, and a cigarette that was not soggy from jungle rains.

It was 39 months since Heinz disembarked the ship in Australia. He had seen areas of the world he'd never imagined he would see. He had lived with physical stress his body was not fully prepared to handle. He had experienced emotional stress that he would seldom talk about, the memory and effect of which would at times debilitate him, and would never completely go away. He had seen things in the war that made no sense at all. He had seen both the strength and the weakness of human beings, and had witnessed unbelievable courage and embarrassing cowardice.

Time to Go Home

He'd served with great leaders and with those who left a lot to be desired. He was proud, and yet hurt at the same time. Heinz naturally had regrets and memories of horrible things and scenes he never wanted to see again. However, complaining about what he had experienced was not something that Heinz would do. He remained committed to his country: the United States of America. Like his fellow soldiers all over the world, he had wondered from time to time why it was necessary for young men to go off to war; and sometimes the strategies of the commanders directing the war efforts didn't seem wise to Heinz. Despite his doubts, he never claimed the kind of expertise that would allow him to comment. "All that I was asked to do was to be part of an important team and to do my part as well as I possibly could," he declared. "I was never hired to make the big decisions, and I am eternally grateful that I was not called upon to do so." Heinz wasn't naïve; in fact, his outlook on life demanded respect, loyalty, integrity—and the chance to move on. Some of those who served with Heinz, and many who served in other theaters, would never be able to shake the war, reliving and frequently recounting their war experiences.

Although Heinz was able to step beyond that to live a life largely uncluttered by an obsession with his time in combat, he never stopped praying for peace. He recalled reading something General Douglas MacArthur said many years after the war, at West Point in 1962. General MacArthur, at age 82, commented upon conditions that soldiers in World War II experienced:

> ". . . against the filth of dirty foxholes, the stench of ghostly trenches, the slime of dripping dugouts, those boiling suns of relentless heat, those torrential rains of devastating storms, the loneliness and utter desolation of jungle trails, the bitterness of long separation of those they loved and cherished, the deadly pestilence of tropic disease, the horror of stricken areas of war..." In the speech's conclusion, the General remarked, "The soldier, above all other people, prays for peace."

There would be reminders of the 32nd Division after Heinz returned home, but many of the reminders were simply tributes to those who had served as part of the Red Arrow Division. Wisconsin Highway 32 was named the *Red Arrow Highway* in honor of the 32nd Division. A Wisconsin state statute established this commemoration:

> **Wisconsin Statute 84. 104 32nd Division Memorial Highway.** In order to commemorate the 32nd Infantry Division, also known as The Red Arrow Division, which, while composed mainly of men from Wisconsin, Illinois and Michigan, brought fame and glory to these states during World Wars I and II by their sacrifice, devotion and bravery and which is now established as a Wiscon-

Time to Go Home

sin national guard division, the department is directed to establish a highway memorial designated route 32 by renumbering certain existing highways linking Illinois and Michigan through Wisconsin. Beginning at the Illinois-Wisconsin state line renumber state trunk highway 42 to a point where it joins the present Wisconsin state trunk highway 32 at Sheboygan; continuing over the present Wisconsin state trunk highway 32 north to the junction with U. S. highway 8 at Laona; continuing over the present Wisconsin state trunk highway 32 north to junction with U. S. highway 45 at Three Lakes; thence north on U. S. highway 45 to Michigan-Wisconsin state line at Land O'Lakes. The department is further directed that in addition to the numeral 32, the highway markers on this highway carry a red arrow, and that historical

Highway 32 in northern Wisconsin as it meanders through the Chequamegon National Forest.

markers be erected and maintained along the highway in honor of the 32nd Division and its members.

A new park in Milwaukee was named the Red Arrow Park. Later, because of interstate highway construction, the original park location was lost, but the park was relocated to a downtown Milwaukee location. On Veterans Day, 1984, a new granite monument in the shape of the Red Arrow insignia was dedicated at the relocated Red Arrow Park.

Knowing that the monument to the 32nd is in Milwaukee has been a nice thought for Heinz. After all, he not only served with the 32nd, but also served for many years in Milwaukee law enforcement. Still, the red arrow symbol brings back less-than-pleasant memories. Heinz has been known to tear up at the sight of the red arrow. "A lot of people with the red arrow patch on their uniforms died," says Heinz. "That's what we need to remember. It's a symbol of convincing victories. It is also a symbol of many who sacrificed their lives."

There is a memorial in the Philippines, as well. Its inscription reads:

> Erected by the officers and men of the 32nd Infantry Division United States Army in memory of their gallant comrades who were killed along the Villa Verde Trail.

At this time in his life, Heinz was heading home.

Time to Go Home

Monument to the 32nd Red Arrow Division,
Red Arrow Park, Milwaukee.

One of the recurring thoughts during the trip was about Caroline, who had been so faithful in remembering him and staying in touch with him while he was away. Still, he had no idea exactly what it would be like when he returned. The ship arrived in San Francisco on July 13, 1945, seven days before his formal discharge from active duty. Heinz and some of his shipmates boarded trains bound for their home destinations. "Hey, guys, I'm going to miss you," shouted Heinz . . . "but not a whole lot."

"*Likewise*," came the response.

Heinz did stay in touch for awhile with a number of the soldiers who were from the Milwaukee area, but over time, the war became a distant and fading chapter in their lives. Life after the war consumed most of their thoughts and energies.

The train from San Francisco arrived in Chicago on a Thursday evening. Heinz and another soldier, Julian (known to his friends as Juli) who lived in Green Bay, were dropped off at Fort Sheridan. While they waited to make connections to Milwaukee and Green Bay, they stopped by the fort's "watering hole."

As they sipped a beer, they couldn't help but overhear the conversation going on among a number of young army recruits. For the most part, the conversation was about how hard they had it in basic training. "How can they expect so much from us?" asked one of the recruits.

Time to Go Home

"Yah, I can't think of anything worse than this," said another.

"What do they expect of us? This is just unfair."

Heinz and Juli were amused by the conversation, but thought these young guys needed to realize that things could be a lot worse. The older men wore jackets that covered up their army shirts—shirts that held stripes and medals and other clear indications that they had served in the war. Juli stood up where he could be easily seen, and with a slightly raised voice said, "Heinz, are you warm? I think we ought to take our jackets off." So Heinz stood up, too, and both of them took off their jackets, revealing to the recruits that these two had seen much rougher times. Without saying anything, the two sat down. The room became quiet, until one of the recruits apologized for possibly offending the seasoned soldiers. Another offered to buy Heinz and Juli a drink, and then others in the room offered to do the same.

"Everything is relative," says Heinz. "Oftentimes we think we are in impossible situations, only to discover later that those situations were really quite easy compared to some of the situations encountered out in the world." Of course, for Heinz and Juli, the war was over. They had no desire to get into any kind of war of words with the recruits, and the recruits, it appeared, felt the same way.

PUFF

Heinz still had to make his way to Milwaukee, but he was beginning to feel as if he really was going to be home. He had called his father, who would be there to greet him when he arrived in Milwaukee. When he arrived, the reunion with his father was a joyous moment, indeed. Heinz loved his father. There was so much to discuss—a lot of catching up to do. For the moment, however, those things could wait. "We'll have time to talk one of these days," said Heinz. "But, for now, it's just nice to be back. Let's get a beer." And that's exactly what they did.

Jobs were not easy to come by when Heinz returned, but he was not afraid to work. For an hourly wage of 42 cents, he took a job in a gravel pit. It was physical labor, but after his time in the military, he was in pretty good shape. Fortunately, the work in the gravel pit didn't last long. Heinz managed to get a job in a tool and die apprenticeship with Globe Union in Milwaukee, which was a much better job. It provided a few more resources and a bit more time for some social activities. He dated a few young women, but nothing even came close to a serious, long-lasting relationship.

Before long, he made his way back to one of his old neighborhoods—the place where he had first met Caroline. It was a weekday morning when he knocked on the door of Caroline's house. Her mother greeted

Heinz at the door and told him that Caroline was working at a nearby bank.

Heinz got there just before lunchtime. It had been a long time and he was just a little nervous. Had Caroline changed or become attached to someone? As soon as he saw her, however, he relaxed. Caroline was thrilled to see him. They had lunch together and it didn't take long to become reacquainted because, after all, they had known each other for many years.

As with most close friendships, Heinz and Caroline were able to pick up where they left off more than four years earlier, even though they were considerably more mature now. Canceling out the passage of time seemed to be a mark of true and lasting friendships—it didn't matter how much time had passed; when the friends were together, it was as if they had never been apart.

Heinz later admitted that he had gotten a small amount of prompting from his father, who thought the world of Caroline and prayed that she would one day be his daughter-in-law. Heinz had already been anxious to reconnect with Caroline, but his father's encouragement gave him another reason to do so.

"I asked her for a date," Heinz recalled, "and she agreed. Then, after that date I thought it was a waste of time to engage in a lengthy courtship, so I asked her to marry me." At least no one could have accused Heinz of being indecisive.

Luckily, Caroline said "yes," What about the other dates Heinz had had after returning from the war? Caroline later said "Heinz made the rounds a bit, just to remove any doubt in his mind that I was the absolute best of all possibilities."

In October of 1945, life was looking up for many people in the United States. The war was over and it was a new day. Heinz and Caroline's wedding was scheduled to take place in September of the next year.

Caroline was a wonderful, attractive young woman with talents to match. She had a good job at First Wisconsin National Bank, but her real love and abilities were in music. She had a beautiful singing voice and had received some professional training. She was able to use her voice in a variety of settings during the war. Some individuals who could distinguish and appreciate a unique and highly-qualified voice even suggested that she would be an excellent candidate for Julliard.

Though Caroline could easily have pursued a career in music, at the time it was just an avocation. "Most of the boys were off at war," Caroline said, "and music was a great way to pass the time and fill some of the hours when I was not at work." Also, she had a very fine relationship with her parents and enjoyed spending time with them. According to Heinz, Caroline's father "spoiled her something awful, which simply meant I had big shoes to fill."

Caroline performed with the Milwaukee Civic Light Opera Company. This performing group was funded, in part, by the city of Milwaukee. She was trained in vocal music by a professional voice teacher. "It cost most of my disposable income to do that," she said, "but I thought it was worth it and I really enjoyed it."

After Heinz and Caroline became engaged, the Civic Light Opera Company attempted to recruit Heinz to participate in operas, as well. "I'm sure they did it to keep Caroline performing," he said. "I had little to offer, although I did agree to take a role in one of the operas the company performed."

After that, the company offered him another role, this one requiring that he wear tights. "Are you kidding me," Heinz recalled himself saying at the time. "After spending 39 months in and out of jungles fighting a war, you want me to appear in public wearing tights? No way!" There may have been a lot of things Heinz would do for Caroline, but this was not one of them.

Upon agreeing to marry Heinz, Caroline's thoughts of music and performing were relegated to second place. The money she was spending for a music teacher could now be saved for an upcoming wedding, so she left the opera company and dropped the voice lessons.

But she never gave up her love for music. She sang in Lutheran church choirs for a while, but even backed away from that when the children came. She sang for many weddings. "I enjoyed that," said Caroline, "but more importantly, it was a way to get a few bucks to supplement the family budget."

Few people who have known her in the later years of her life even know that she was once a rather accomplished accordion player. She liked the instrument so much that when her two children were old enough, both learned to play the accordion. And singing, for any reason at all, was a characteristic of Caroline. She sang to, and with, the children on a regular basis.

Heinz and Caroline became husband and wife September 28, 1946. Their honeymoon took place

Heinz and Caroline Puff

Time to Go Home

Heinz with young daughter, Carol, in Milwaukee, circa 1947.

close to where they would eventually retire, in the northwoods of Wisconsin. The cottage they rented on Big Arbor Vitae Lake cost $72 for a week, and that included three meals a day.

It was certainly appropriate for this location to have been chosen by Heinz. His love affair with his bride, of course, was destined to last for life. Although he may not have known it at the time, his love affair with a special area of northern Wisconsin was likewise destined to be a life-long affair.

Heinz's job at Globe Union lasted for several years. His work area was close to a window, and Heinz spent many moments of his hours there looking out the window, convinced that there had to be something in the world that would be more satisfying. A number of possibilities frequently rolled through his mind, but one of them almost always rose to the top. It wasn't that he couldn't have stayed with his employer for a long time. It had more to do with pursuing a long held dream.

Eventually, several events at work convinced him to follow his dream, and he began to look for ways to pursue a career goal that he had not shared openly, but that was very important to him.

One of the events that soured Heinz on his current employer involved a co-worker named Walter Hart, who was in his early seventies, but was still very productive on the job, and very knowledgeable in the profession of tool and die making. One day, without warning, Walter was dismissed with no retirement compensation and no pension from his employer. Others at work felt sorry for Walter, and, like Heinz, thought their employer was extremely unfair.

A retirement party was planned for Walter. "We bought him fishing tackle and other things," said Heinz. "We wanted to make him feel good and we wanted to let him know that there were many who appreciated him and his long service to the company.

It was a nice party. And the next day, Walter died."

Heinz couldn't get over the thought that Walter had been so devastated by his forced retirement and seeming lack of appreciation by the company, that it contributed significantly to his death. Heinz was more convinced than ever to think beyond the tool and die world.

III

LIFE ON THE FORCE

It was a different life. Heinz was now a husband and an expectant father. He remained close to his father and to the parents of Caroline. They lived in a flat owned by Caroline's parents. Their first child, a girl, was born during their first year of marriage.

Since the birth took place less than nine months after their wedding, Heinz and Caroline were subjected to some ribbing about "having to get married." Actually, the baby was a preemie – several months early and weighing in at just slightly more than three pounds. Despite that, she was healthy and grew quickly. The proud parents named her Carol.

Less than a year later, Carol's brother, Gary, was born. Now the family seemed almost perfect—a loving couple with a girl and a boy.

Heinz and Caroline were doing just fine with their two little ones, but Heinz was still restless. He wasn't fully comfortable at his work, and he had long dreamed about becoming a state trooper. So, having given up on Globe Union and on being a tool and die maker, he finally decided to do something about his dream. He applied for a trooper position in the state of Wisconsin, with the sheriff's office in Milwaukee County, and with the police department in the city of Milwaukee. After a short period of time, he was called into the city to take some exams. There was one small thing that concerned Heinz—his weight. The police department required a height of 5'10"—Heinz could match that—and a weight for new officers of at least 150 pounds. After having been "shrunk" in the jungles of New Guinea and the Philippines, Heinz would have to add a few pounds to officially qualify. Heinz recalls that there were more than 300 applicants at the time he was applying. So the exams, along with adding a few pounds, were very important factors.

Much to his delight, Heinz was the third one called from the group of applicants to participate in an oral exam. Even Heinz would not have imagined that he would fare so well on the written exam. But now came an even more challenging quest—the personal interview by a number of police officials. It was quite unnerving, being in a room of seasoned police professionals, including police commissioners, who were going to ask all sorts of questions. The question and answer session went quite well and Heinz was pleased.

Life on the Force

The final question came from an older gentleman who hadn't said much. "You served in the military?" he asked.

"Yes sir, that is correct," said Heinz.

"So, do you think the experience you had in the army would help you as a police officer?"

"I don't know exactly," replied Heinz. "I was a fifty-caliber machine gunner. Do you use those around here?"

Everyone in the room laughed. Heinz got the job, and never regretted getting into police work.

After some training, Heinz was sworn in and began working with a veteran officer. His first assignment was a patrol on the midnight to eight a. m. shift. Eventually, with retirements and promotions on the force, he was able to move to the four p. m. to midnight shift. His first assignment during this time slot was on the patrol boat in plain clothes on the Milwaukee River.

His partner on the river was Teddy Meyer. "I'll never forget the night Teddy and I were on the river patrol and noticed up ahead a group of teenagers skinny-dipping in the river. It was dark and we couldn't see too much, but when they noticed our boat, they all scrambled from the river, running right past the place on the shore where they had left their clothes.

"Teddy and I pulled the boat up to the shore at the point where the swimmers had been. We couldn't see any of them, assuming they were hiding someplace away from the shore. And we sat there for a while debating whether or not we should pick up all their clothes as evidence. It was an intriguing and tempting idea, but we decided to give the kids a break and let them have their clothes."

The boat they cruised in the Milwaukee River was a rather powerful ChrisCraft. Years later, when he retired to the lake in northern Wisconsin, he wished he had such a boat. After using it for patrol for some time, he became quite proficient in its operation. Being a true inboard, it was capable of some very tight maneuvers.

Heinz tells of the time a sergeant of his—who always wanted others to think of him as a very tough guy—asked to ride with him on the river to "check things out." Heinz obliged. Before the cruise was over, Heinz treated the sergeant to what has come to be known as a "bat turn"—the ability of an inboard to make a 180-degree turn at full speed without swamping the boat. After that experience, Heinz says, "the sergeant never came back and never asked again to 'check things out.'"

"Another of my partners on the force was a fella named Queeny—an Italian," Heinz recalls. The two of them actually had a lot of fun together. Queeny knew how to find the good Italian restaurants and they managed to have dinner at one place or another during many of their shifts. Most of the restaurants' proprietors refused to take money from them, so, according to Heinz, they always made sure to order the less expensive items on the menu and leave a generous tip.

There are many stories Heinz has to tell about his years as a Milwaukee police officer. Some are more vivid than others.

"As a detective in plain clothes I was once sent to investigate allegations that a certain young girl, about 16 years old, at a local high school was causing some commotion," recounts Heinz. "There were rumors and disruptions concerning her sexual activities with many of the boys in the high school. My investigation showed that the concerns were founded. I worked with the young lady and determined that her home situation was less than favorable. She was scheduled to appear in juvenile court, and I, of course, had to be there since I was the officer involved. I had talked with the young lady prior to the appearance in court and explained what my recommendation would be. She did not object. The judge knew the circumstances from the court documents, and asked me my recommendation. I simply said that I felt it would be best for her to spend her time at the school for delinquent girls in Wisconsin until she turned 18. Without any further discussion, the judge said 'So ordered.' Part of me felt bad for the girl, but I knew this was something that had to be done and I prayed that it would ultimately be to her benefit."

Heinz often found himself hoping that the less confrontational methods would work best and that force would not be necessary. He knew about force. He knew the power of weapons. He carried them and used them for most of his adult life—first in the army and then on the police force. But he did his best to avoid using weapons. As he said, he discovered over and over again that the most powerful weapons a police officer has are his common sense and his mouth. Heinz always referred to his profession as a police officer as a "helping" one. "The job was not about arresting people—although that was sometimes necessary; it was about helping. As I look back, I find the most satisfaction in knowing I was able to be of some help in the lives of people."

"I was called to a home once for an alleged domestic dispute. I entered the home and was told by a father that his 17-year-old son was acting in a violent manner; that he had a baseball bat and was threatening to use it on his father. I asked where the son was and found that he was behind a closed door in his bedroom. He had gone there when he saw the police car pull up. Shouting loudly enough so that he could hear me through the door, I announced who I was and that

I was going to open the door. I did so carefully. And there was the young man, hands clinched on the bat, ready to swing it. I felt that moving toward him or pulling my service revolver would have been overkill. So I just started to talk, asking some simple questions and attempting to calm him down. His grip on the bat loosened. And little by little, I was getting closer to him. Finally I was close enough to grab hold of the bat. The young man resisted, but not very forcefully. The showdown was over.

"But now I had the task of determining what to do next. I did put him in handcuffs. Since he was under the age of 18, I had to ask his father if he wished to have his son taken to court. The father would have to press charges. I could tell the father did not want to do that, but felt the boy should somehow be held accountable. So I took the boy out to the squad car and we talked—quietly, peacefully. The boy was obviously sorry for his actions. He said nothing that would have indicated abuse by his father. In fact, he talked about how much he loved his father.

"We had quite a long conversation, and eventually I was comfortable taking the cuffs off and returning him to his father who was waiting for him in the house. The two embraced and even cried a little. And then I used my mouth weapon one more time—this time a little less peacefully. 'If I ever hear of the slightest bit of trouble at this address again, I will personally see to it that your ass ends up in the can,' I said."

Heinz had children of his own. He often prayed that they would mature into responsible and law-abiding citizens. Also, he knew that his work heightened the risk that they could grow up without a father. At times, the prospect of leaving Caroline alone to raise the children was a most unpleasant thought. He didn't think too much about the negative possibilities, but the reality was still there.

Heinz and Caroline loved their children and enjoyed spending time with them. There were the usual family, sports, and school activities. When Gary was old enough, Heinz introduced him to Boy Scouts. Heinz became a troop leader so that he and Gary could spend more time together. He felt that the skills and discipline taught through scout activity would be good for Gary. Having served in the military, Heinz had an even greater appreciation for some of the things that could be learned through scouting. A favorite memory of Heinz is when his troop took top honors at a Boy Scout Jamboree for a flag presentation marching event taught to the troop by Heinz. And, of course, anything Heinz could do to help his children mature would help in the event that he would no longer be around.

Carol got some of the resolve and discipline from Heinz, too. She would frequently accompany Heinz

Life on the Force

Heinz, Caroline, and children Gary and Carol, in Milwaukee, circa 1954.

and Gary to activities Gary was involved in. In a pick-up baseball game that was short one player to make teams with the same number of players, Heinz encouraged Carol to play. The team to which she was assigned was anything but excited about the prospect of a girl on the team ... until at Carol's first at-bat she hit a home run.

Heinz and Caroline still enjoy telling stories of the time when Gary and Carol were growing up. Gary, especially, inherited his father's and grandfather's love of fishing.

Heinz with his son, Gary, and his father, Arthur.

Heinz and Caroline enjoyed a variety of activities with the children while experiencing the same concerns about their children's behavior and safety as do most parents. For Heinz, the thought that they might grow up without him was always somewhere in the back of his mind.

To be sure, police work did involve some tense, and sometimes physical, struggles that could be life-threatening. "All that time in the army was helpful," Heinz admitted, "even though it was not necessarily pleasant." The physical training and instincts he acquired in the military were very valuable on the force. Action was sometimes necessary, but inappropriate *reaction* could be very damaging. Those who worked with Heinz recognized in him a kind of cool and contemplative demeanor as he went about his work.

Life on the Force

He was not given to outbursts of emotion. Rather, he seemed to quietly process information and calmly determine the best course of action—not that he didn't often feel that his stomach was being tied in knots. There were situations in which he justifiably feared for his life.

During the unsettled 1960s, things seemed to unravel with some regularity. There were upheavals, protests, and political unrest in many parts of the country. Tensions among the races and disagreements over policies of the government related to the Vietnam war and other issues were felt in many communities. Milwaukee was no exception.

Known as the "bloodiest night in Milwaukee history," July 30, 1967, is a date those serving as Milwaukee police officers at the time will always remember. Ironically, that exact date had been declared to be a national day of prayer by then-President Lyndon Johnson. Watts and Detroit had already been the scenes of race riots.

Calls to police stations in Milwaukee began late in the evening of July 30. Crowds were gathering, rocks were being thrown, stores were being looted, and fires were being set. In the hours that followed, the city erupted with violence. The most intense time was July 30 and 31, but it took even longer for the riots to be completely quelled.

PUFF

It was around 11:30 at night on the 30th that the phone rang at the Puff household. "Report immediately in full uniform," was the command from the sergeant on the phone. That's strange, thought Heinz, but he responded immediately. At the precinct he was told of race riots that were breaking out around town. He and a partner, Gary, were taken up to Green Bay Avenue in the vicinity of a jewelry store and Kess Arms, a gun shop.

The concern, of course, was that there had not been an opportunity to clean out the gun shop. It was full of weapons and ammunition. Store windows were already being broken in other parts of the city and looting was in full force. The arms store needed to be protected. Two of his fellow officers were stationed behind the store, and Heinz and his partner were assigned to protect the front of the store.

It was not customary for an officer to carry a 12-gauge shotgun, but on this assignment, Heinz was given one. He was told by his superior to stand in front of the store. There was a big light in front of the store which would have thoroughly illuminated Heinz. He would have been a target in the spotlight, not to mention that the alarm on the jewelry store was blaring. Heinz would have been clearly identified not only by the light, but by the sound.

Heinz surveyed the situation. Across the street

Life on the Force

was a Chinese restaurant and in front of the restaurant there was a brick planter standing several feet high. This seemed to Heinz to be a much better place to watch the front of the gun shop.

After just a short time in his position in front of the restaurant, the alarm on the jewelry store was getting quite annoying. Heinz called to ask if the alarm could be turned off. No, unfortunately, was the response. The owner of the jewelry store had been called, but was afraid to come to the store to turn the alarm off. "Do you want me to turn it off?" Heinz asked.

"Sure, you can do that if you know how to turn it off," came the reply. So, with that official okay, Heinz aimed his 12-gauge shotgun at the large bell on the outside of the store and blew it off the wall. No more annoying alarm. And for a period of time, it was quiet on Green Bay Avenue.

The record of police radio calls on July 30 and July 31, 1967, showed a growing avalanche of dangerous activity throughout Milwaukee. There were reports of rioters breaking store windows, looting, fires being set, rioters throwing stones at passing cars, shootings, burglaries, beatings, and growing numbers of moving mobs. The first call of looting came in at 11:35 PM on July 30. It came from a Goodyear store on West Fond du Lac Avenue. A number of calls followed before midnight, of rioters starting fires. At 11:51

the department received an unconfirmed report of a squad car being tipped over, and at 11:56 the report of a man shot at 3rd and Vine. Distraught residents kept calling, and the volume of calls increased until nearly 4:00 AM. The police requested additional personnel and munitions. The sheriff's office was notified and staff members of the sheriff's office were summoned. Also, the sheriff's office was asked to quickly bring in a supply of hard helmets. Reports of injuries were increasing. Hospitals were notified and emergency personnel were called to assist. Burglar alarms were sounding around the city. Liquor stores and jewelry stores were being targeted. At 2:12 AM on July 31 came the report of a police officer being shot. Reports of fires came in with frightening regularity.

In many instances, the firehouses were not equipped for the volume of calls and were unable to get to some of the fires. Ambulances were in short supply, and many, like the firefighters, had problems getting to the locations where there were injuries. Several reports came in of firemen being pinned down by sniper fire. As the minutes in the early morning hours of July 31 passed, the violence and destruction increased.

At around two in the morning, Heinz and his partner could hear the approaching sound of riotous voices and the sounds of property destruction on Green Bay Avenue. When Heinz could finally see what all the noise was about, it was intimidating to say the least. From sidewalk to sidewalk and all across the street was this moving mass of humanity.

The closer the people in the crowd got, the more apparent it became that most of them were young—teenagers and young adults. They seemed to delight in smashing windows and looting any appealing items they discovered in the retail establishments.

At this point, Heinz and his partner left the relative safety of the brick planter in front of the Chinese restaurant and took a very visible position in the middle of the street. It didn't deter them a bit. The crowd grew larger in size as it got closer, moving ever forward. There wasn't a whole lot of time to think, but Heinz was faced with a major dilemma. Could he possibly fire into a crowd of mostly young people? Could he run the risk of being injured, perhaps killed? And what about his weapons and those in the gun shop? They could be taken and used for even more violent activity by members of the crowd.

"What do we do?" was the nervous question of his partner. Time was running out. "If they get past us," his partner said, "we're dead." Even the brick planter would have provided no cover or consolation. Without a lengthy discussion about the options, Heinz determined quietly to try to warn the crowd without causing what could have been unnecessary injury.

He reloaded the chamber he had emptied taking out the bell, pumped the shotgun, raised it in the air, and aimed high over the heads of the encroaching crowd. If this doesn't work, thought Heinz, the second shot may have to be leveled at human beings. God, I hope that's not going to be necessary, thought Heinz.

The shot rang out. "And by the grace of God," Heinz said later, "all I saw after that shot rang out were behinds and elbows, and we never saw another person at that location on Green Bay Avenue all night."

Heinz looked at Gary and Gary looked at Heinz. They were looks of relative relief, mixed with a tinge of leftover panic. "Man, do you realize what could have happened?" Gary asked. "Yes, I'm afraid I know," said Heinz. Things were still uncertain, so they stood their ground until daybreak when they were relieved of their duty at that location.

When a sergeant arrived to get a report, he couldn't help but notice that the gun shop, jewelry store and Chinese restaurant still had windows.

He said, "Well, I'm glad they didn't get this far. Did you see them at all?"

"Actually, we did," replied Heinz, but you're right, they didn't get this far."

"You're very lucky," said the Sergeant

"Yes, indeed," said Heinz. Later Heinz would reflect on that night on Green Bay Avenue. He summed it up with just a few small phrases: "I took two shots. Both quieted things down. No one was hurt."

Not everyone was as "lucky" as Heinz and Gary. A number of people lost their lives as a result of the riots. According to some reports, the death of a police detective and a person being investigated helped set off the riots. The mayor of Milwaukee at the time was Henry Maier. He quickly brought in the National Guard and declared martial law. The worst was over within 24 hours, but the police had to be vigilant in the aftermath.

For a period of time, Heinz and his partner were assigned to patrol an area hardest hit by the riots—out Wisconsin Avenue from downtown, up to Vliet Street, and over to Fond Du Lac Avenue. Four officers were assigned to each patrol car, and two of the occupants were armed with shotguns, a weapon not unfamiliar to Heinz.

Heinz saw another 50-caliber machine gun, too. He hadn't been close to one of those since the war. In addition to the police patrols following the riots, National Guard soldiers were patrolling the streets of Milwaukee in jeeps outfitted with the machine guns. Heinz doesn't recall that the guns were ever used in Milwaukee, but they did send a strong message to those who may have been inclined to resurrect the riots.

A rare undercover operation that comes to his mind

involved a sting on prostitution. He was assigned to a particular neighborhood bar. He stopped by, walked in, and sat down at the bar. He was in plain clothes, of course. It was early afternoon. He had a beer and engaged in a bit of small talk with the bartender. Sitting alone at a table near the bar was a woman who was not really occupied—just waiting, it appeared, for something to do. He had been told that single women just sitting in the bar area might be those who engaged in prostitution. After looking at her and sharing a smile with her several times, she came and sat down next to him. They exchanged a "Hello, how are you today?" After a short time, she asked if he would like to go upstairs with her. He consented. He then followed her to an apartment above the tavern where the "cost" was discussed. He agreed to the price and she excused herself to get ready. At that point he introduced himself as an undercover Milwaukee police officer and made the arrest. She was escorted to his automobile and he drove her to the police station for booking.

"I didn't like having to arrest her," he said. "I really wished she had chosen a different line of work. There were many things I didn't really appreciate in law enforcement, but this was one I really didn't like. It destroys those who put themselves up for sale as well as many who patronize them."

When Caroline heard just a little of the event, she

liked it even less than Heinz did. When Heinz got home from working his shift that day, he offered to take Caroline out. Working undercover at the time, he drove his nice, relatively new unmarked Pontiac. Normally, Heinz did not talk about his work. Caroline didn't need to be burdened and much of what Heinz did had an element of confidentiality.

However, that day Caroline asked how his work had gone, and he mentioned that he had to arrest a prostitute and take her to the station. "In your car?" Caroline asked. And before she would get in the car again for any reason, she sprayed the entire interior of the car with Lysol.

One night, quite late, there was a knock on the door at his home. He remembers opening the door to see a young man and a young woman. He didn't recognize either of them. The young woman said, "You're Officer Puff."

As it was late at night, Heinz recalls saying to himself, *oh shit, maybe I should have gotten my gun. Maybe this is someone I once arrested seeking to get even.*

"Yes, I'm Officer Puff," Heinz said. "What can I do for you?"

"You may not remember me," the young woman said. But as soon as she mentioned her name, Heinz remembered. It was the girl he had recommended be placed in the girl's school. At that point, Heinz still wasn't sure why she was stopping by and not sure what she may be intending to do.

"I just had to find you to say thanks for what you did for me," she said. "It was the best thing that could have happened to me."

"Well, come on in for a minute," Heinz said. And they talked for a while. She talked a bit about her parents, who never really cared for her, and how she had chosen to do things that made her feel loved and accepted, even though those things were wrong.

"But that's all behind me now," she said. "I'm very optimistic about the future. This young man is my fiancé. We have great plans for the future, and I owe so much of that to you."

"The experience was one of those 'it made it all worth it' experiences," said Heinz. "I don't think my body actually hit the mattress that night. I was floating."

So much of what a police officer does makes people angry. Understandably, people resent being questioned, arrested, fined, and even sent to prison. "But to see some examples of good coming from what I did as a police officer is heartening," admitted Heinz, who is not given to very public displays of emotion. "I pray there were many other positive results like this one, even though I will never know about them."

Heinz always thought that just as her visit was

not about getting even, police work is not about that, either. Oh, there were some police officers who were "pumped" about the power they had—the chance to make those who broke the law pay and to show them who was in charge. For the most part, those officers were never very happy. For some, the profession simply afforded the opportunity to live out a mean streak that was deep within them. Perhaps, Heinz thought, it was some basic insecurity or personal inferiority that drove them, as if they gained relief from their own feelings about themselves by demonstrating powerful superiority over others.

But if an officer could somehow help bring some sanity and normalcy to the lives of individuals—change their direction—and in the process, make the world a better and safer place to be, that was the biggest reward that could be afforded. The job was not about personally *proving* anything. It was about helping to make a positive difference.

Heinz spent some 25 years as a police officer in Milwaukee. He worked foot patrol, squad cars, and plain clothes detective assignments. He worked in high crime areas, quieter suburban areas, and on every possible shift. He enjoyed the detective work the most. At one point in his career he was up for permanent assignment to a detective position, but lost out to the son of a high-ranking police official. "It's okay," said

Heinz. "There are politics in any profession. I was happy to serve, in whatever capacity, and I'm grateful that I survived."

The family, of course, participated in his profession, too. They became accustomed to his changing work schedule and the times he was called in to work on short notice. It was a way of life; and everyone in the family accepted and supported it.

Heinz tells the story of one incident involving his young son that could have raised a few eyebrows. He left hurriedly for work one day while still doing the river patrol assignment, and discovered when he reached the boathouse that he had left his gun at home. He called home immediately and asked Caroline to bring him his gun. Their young son, Gary, was home at the time and Caroline had to take him along. Since Caroline did not drive, they took public transportation. On a bus, one of Gary's young friends was a passenger, as well. And the friend shouted across the bus to Gary, "Hey Gary, where are you going?" to which Gary replied, "To take Daddy a gun."

An example of the commitment Heinz had to his profession involved a time when most of his fellow police officers contracted the "blue flu." Heinz chose not to "get sick" but rather stayed on the force and performed his duty. "When I took my oath as a police officer, I promised to serve. I don't recall promising to serve *unless* I determined that the pay or benefits were insufficient. How could I *not* fulfill my obligation? I took an oath to serve."

When the force was restored to "health," Heinz and the others who had continued to work were shunned by those who had not worked. "I recall a fellow officer confiding in me that he had been strongly encouraged not to talk with me.

"I remember the captain asking me if I should be assigned in such a way as to avoid contact with those who were upset with my behavior. And I said, 'of course not.' I was not ashamed of the position I had taken.

"In time, it seemed that all was forgotten. Friendships were restored. In fact, later on, I recall a number of the flu victims saying that they had a new level of respect for me, even though they may have still disagreed with the position I took. I'll always feel good about honoring my oath to serve."

IV

THE PRODIGAL PUFF

For many years of his early adult life, concern about his older brother, Gerhard, was never far from Heinz's consciousness. From little on, Gerhard seemed to choose the wrong way to get things done. He had an obsession for getting things on the "five finger discount." Heinz recalls the first run-in Gerhard had with the law—a disorderly conduct charge when Heinz was only ten years old. When Heinz was a teenager, Gerhard was charged with a number of crimes, including stealing and assaulting a guard in the reformatory to which he had been sent. Later he was incarcerated for burglary, car theft, and for a prison escape.

When Heinz returned from the war and sought employment, he was declined several times because his older brother had worked at those places and had been fired for stealing. That horrible habit just escalated as Gerhard got older. He served short sentences in prison on several occasions. All of this seemed in such contrast to the work of his brother. Gerhard was determined to break the law. Heinz was determined to uphold it. Conversations between the two never got too far. Heinz loved his brother, but he could never convince him to give up his wayward ways.

Caroline even tried on numerous occasions. "Gerhard," she would say, "you can have all those things you want. You can have a nice, new, fancy car. You can get a job, work hard, save your money, and buy a nice car or nice clothes or whatever." And Gerhard would respond in a way that made it appear that Caroline was living in a totally different world. "Why would I want to work for all those things when it's so easy to get them for nothing?"

Heinz has no idea if the era in which Gerhard was a teenager had anything to do with his fascination with criminal activity. Gerhard was a teenager when names such as John Dillinger, Baby Face Nelson, Al Capone, and Dutch Schultz were quite well known. Dillinger and other crime bosses garnered so much press in the late 1920s and early 1930s, they became glamorized. Those were the years of the great Depression and prohibition. After the stock market crash in 1929, there wasn't a lot of love for banks and bank robbers were often seen as modern day Robin Hoods. Whether or not the gangster era influenced Gerhard, he was certainly aware of those high profile criminals. Gerhard was twenty when John Dillinger was killed.

Gerhard, like his brother Heinz, was a handsome, slender young man with lots of dark, wavy hair. It wasn't difficult for him to attract young women. He was a good dancer. He liked the latest in fashionable clothing. He was very fond of big automobiles. He followed sports. And he developed a passion for gambling. For Gerhard, none of these "loves" of his could be accommodated without taking them or taking the money to buy them.

Gerhard had accumulated quite a list of run-ins with the law. His first arrest for disorderly conduct came at the young age of twenty. His first sentence to the Wisconsin State Penitentiary came just a little over a year later, in August of 1935, for stealing animals. This was hardly a violent crime, but taking things that did not belong to him would become a pattern. If he could sell what he had taken, or use it in some way to his benefit, that's all that seemed to matter. Late in 1935, he was transferred to the state reformatory at Green Bay, Wisconsin. While in Green Bay, he assaulted a guard and was sentenced to an additional term of one to ten years. Following this sentence, he was sent back to the Wisconsin State Penitentiary. Gerhard was released from the state pen on May 24, 1939 and managed to remain a free man for more than three years. It was at the end of 1942 that he again saw the inside of the state penitentiary. This time, he was convicted of attempted armed robbery and sentenced to one to nine years.

Gerhard was a free man when Heinz went off to war, but was back in prison when Heinz returned to Milwaukee from his military service. Gerhard's most recent conviction included the term *armed*. Heinz was horrified. "One thing I worried most about was guns," said Heinz. There was no evidence that Gerhard had graduated to weapons. There were incidents of burglary and robbery, but never armed robbery or burglary. "Guns may have been a way of life for me," said Heinz, "but for Gerhard, they could easily be a way of death."

There were even times when Heinz wondered about the safety of his own guns. After he became a police officer, Heinz wondered if Gerhard would try to lift one of Heinz's guns or a service revolver, if he was freed from prison and chose to visit Heinz and Caroline. Heinz continued to believe that Gerhard would not go that far. Still, it was obvious that all the pleading with Gerhard to stay away from guns had gone unheeded.

On September 6, 1945, not long after Heinz returned from his service in World War II, Gerhard escaped from the penitentiary. This time, freedom was short-lived. Just two weeks after his escape, he was captured in a stolen car and returned to prison for another two years. After being discharged in November 1947, he was again arrested in June 1948. This time it was for breaking and entering a warehouse in Beaver Dam, Wisconsin. Gerhard simply could not avoid activity that put him behind bars.

There were relatively long periods of time when Heinz and Caroline and Heinz's father would not see or hear from Gerhard, but concern for him and prayers for his turn-around never waned. After so many years of his life spent in prison, would he finally decide that there was a better way? Heinz and Caroline certainly hoped so. In between his stints in prison, Gerhard always seemed to find jobs. He was smart and capable in so many ways that could have been rewarding if he could have avoided sinking repeatedly into crime. He drove a truck, worked on a farm, and was a machinist's helper, as well as various other employment. But the income from jobs he was able to find could not bring him the lifestyle he longed to have. For whatever reason, despite being caught numerous times, he always ventured back into crime, believing that next time he would be able to get away with it and live the good life on the outside of the prison walls.

Having served time for his most recent offenses, Gerhard was released from prison on April 25, 1951.

It wasn't long before word began to trickle in that Gerhard had truly taken a major wrong turn. There were news reports of an armed robbery in a Milwaukee doctor's office just a week after his release. The doctor who was robbed identified Gerhard's photo. Gerhard was captured and placed in the Milwaukee County Jail. Among other things, this arrest confirmed his clear movement toward deadly force with the use of a gun.

During this time in jail, he met a fellow inmate with whom he had a lot in common. They both had the middle name Arthur, but the consequential commonality had to do with their fascination with appropriating things that did not belong to them, living the high life on other people's money, and attracting pretty women. The cellmate's name was George Arthur Heroux, someone that Heinz and Caroline did not know, and never got to know. George was not a Milwaukeean but hailed from Rhode Island. He was described in some reports as "a sullen, gun-crazy youth." When they shared cell time, Gerhard was 37 years old. George was only 21.

Bail for Gerhard on the armed robbery charge was set at $3,000. On October 17, 1951, Gerhard was bailed out of the Milwaukee County Jail. The money came from a bail bondsman in Chicago. Some in law enforcement speculated that the bail was arranged by George, who had been released earlier. Gerhard was to

The Prodigal Puff

report for trail on November 15, but never showed up. He was now a fugitive, and along with a partner, George Heroux, his life of crime was about to escalate. Before he met George, Gerhard seemed to be content to operate alone. But now it was a team, and the risk grew proportionately. Gerhard and George quickly became high-level wanted men. The two were the chief suspects in the robbery of the Johnson County National Bank and Trust Company in Prairie Village, Kansas. The robbery took place on October 25, just one week after Gerhard jumped bail.

Reports indicated that the duo of Gerhard and George forced an arriving bank employee to open the front door of the bank just minutes after 8:00 in the morning. One gathered the employees already on the job to a reception area and stood guard over them. All of them were very frightened and willing to follow instructions. Meanwhile, the other of the duo forced a cashier to open the bank's vault. Gerhard and George left the bank about a half hour after entering it, their mission accomplished.

The bank robbery netted Gerhard and George some $62,000, plus traveler's checks and a number of other items that could, in theory, be turned into cash. They left the bank in a car they had stolen several weeks earlier in Tulsa, Oklahoma. It had license plates that had been taken from a car in Hollister, Missouri.

George Arthur Heroux
(photo from FBI website)

Gerhard Arthur Puff
(photo from FBI website)

The car was quickly abandoned following the robbery, but how the two escaped after that is still a mystery. Gerhard and George were the prime suspects in the bank robbery. Because of the seriousness of the crime, the The Federal Bureau of Investigation was now especially interested in the two men. In December 1951, George Heroux was placed on the FBI's *Ten Most Wanted List.*

In 1951, the "Ten Most Wanted Fugitives List" was quite new. It began just a year earlier following publicity disseminated by the FBI about the "toughest guys" the Bureau was seeking to capture. FBI Director J. Edgar Hoover established the list in March, 1950. George was among the early members of a small group of dishonored individuals in the United States who landed in the annals of the Ten Most Wanted history.

The Prodigal Puff

His name was added December 19, 1951. Gerhard's name would be added shortly thereafter, on January 28, 1952.

On January 28, 1952, the United Press issued a story that was picked up and carried by a number of newspapers. Under the title "Gerhard Puff Put on FBI's 'Wanted' list," the story read:

> German born Gerhard Arthur Puff, 37-year-old former convict, was placed today on the FBI's "10 Most Wanted" fugitives.
>
> Puff has been identified as one of two men involved in the $62,000 holdup of a Prairie Valley, Kans., bank. George Arthur Heroux, also charged with being involved in the bank holdup as well as another in which he lone-wolfed, was placed on the list Dec. 19. He still is sought.

The United Press story went on to give more detail on the Kansas robbery and the number of convictions already on the books for both Gerhard Puff and George Heroux. Also, it commented on Gerhard as follows:

> The 150-pound, 5-foot, 10-inch ex-convict was described by the FBI as one proud of his physique, appearance and strength. He is fond of expensive clothes, big automobiles, sports, dancing and gambling.

The article concluded with these words: *The FBI warned that Puff could be "considered extremely dangerous."*

Heinz abhorred his brother's new distinction of being on the Ten Most Wanted list. He had devoted his life to keeping the law. His brother had shown over and over again his intent to break it. What was so different about their backgrounds? How could two brothers with similar influences early in life choose such divergent paths? What had Heinz missed? What could he have done? So many of the early warning signs were probably unknown to Heinz. Gerhard was older, and Heinz was too young in the early days of Gerhard's wanderings to know exactly what they were, much less do anything about them. At times, Heinz even wondered why he was never inclined to engage in the kind of behavior that marked his older brother. Sometimes younger children do follow the example of older siblings. The variety of questions could never be satisfactorily answered.

One of the "crazy" thoughts Heinz had was connected in a small way to the northwoods of Wisconsin that he had come to love. His brother was old enough, and perhaps impressionable enough, in the 1930s to be influenced by the "glamour" of the well-known gangsters of the day. One was John Dillinger, a name well-known to this day. The 2010 movie, "Public Enemies," starring Johnny Depp, revived the story of John Dillinger. The chronicle of Dillinger's life of crime recounts his frequent visits to northern Wisconsin. The famous shoot-out at the Little Bohemia Resort, portrayed in some detail in the 2010 movie, took place just miles from where Heinz and Carol settled in retirement. To some, Dillinger was a "rich and famous" character, to be emulated by others, who proved over and over again his ability to elude the law and live an exciting life.

Could Gerhard have been influenced by the likes of Dillinger in his teenage years? Interestingly, Dillinger and Gerhard were both of German descent, and Gerhard's first arrest came in 1934, the year Dillinger's life ended on the streets of Chicago. Heinz wondered if there could possibly be any connection. Of course, there was no way to go back, and precious little that could change the previous twenty years.

The pain of the choices his brother made was devastating to Heinz personally. They were lasting. And they were mostly personal. But there was some pain professionally, too. Heinz's fellow police officers were aware of Gerhard. It was difficult for some of them to reconcile the connection between the Heinz they knew and the Gerhard whose reputation and actions were such a world apart.

Heinz didn't talk much about his brother then or at any time thereafter. There was no value in explaining, defending, rationalizing, or belittling. There was little value in apologizing for Gerhard. He couldn't understand and he could never find an appropriate way to express his feelings. But Gerhard was still his brother. Nothing could erase that fact. He didn't allude to it very publicly, but he identified with something he once heard said about Jesus—that Jesus hated the sins, but loved the sinner. That love was about to be tested again. And the pain felt by Heinz this time would be even more profound.

Some seven months after Gerhard was placed on the FBI's most wanted list, the FBI was successful in locating him. The FBI was on the trail of both George Heroux and Gerhard. There was no evidence that the two were still together, and there were no substantial leads. Finding George Heroux came first. He was apprehended on July 25, 1952, in Miami, Florida. As a result of his interrogation, FBI agents were able to glean from Heroux the possible whereabouts of Gerhard. The information led FBI agents to a hotel in New York City. The FBI's account of what happened includes the following:

> From clues gained through the apprehension of Puff's criminal associate it was determined that Puff might attempt to make contact with persons at a certain hotel in New York City. During the night and morning of July 25-26, 1952, therefore, FBI agents set up a surveillance at this hotel. Agents were strategically located in the lobby of the hotel, in rooms on the ninth floor, at the hotel entrance, and in the streets surrounding the hotel while FBI radio cars cruised in the vicinity.

The Prodigal Puff

The room under observation, Room 904, was registered to a "John Hanson." Another room had been vacated that day by a man named "J. Burns." Hotel employees identified Burns as Gerhard Arthur Puff. It was felt Puff might attempt to contact Hanson with whom he was friendly. In substantiation of this a note was found on the bed in Room 904 indicating that "Burns" desired to contact Hanson that night or the following morning.

At approximately 9:00 a. m. on the morning of July 26, a new shift of special agents replaced the group on duty in the hotel. Special Agent Joseph John Brock, 44, married and the father of three children, was placed in charge of this group and he and two other agents were stationed in the hotel lobby.

Shortly before noon two girls visited Room 904, then left the hotel. Special agents in radio cars followed them to another hotel. At 1:20 p. m. , they returned to the first hotel and again went to Room 904.

Within a few minutes an individual resembling Puff entered the hotel. After making a telephone call to Room 904 he went up to the room in the elevator. The hotel clerk confirmed the fact that the individual was Puff, and agents were alerted.

It was decided to wait for Puff to return to the lobby before arresting him. Special Agent Brock took up a position at the foot of a small stairway.

Puff did not remain at Room 904 but returned to the first floor in a few minutes by the stairway where Agent Brock was stationed. Puff encountered Agent

Brock, shot him twice in the chest, took his gun, then with a gun in each hand, Puff made a zig-zagging dash through the lobby, firing another shot at converging agents. Agents outside the hotel called to Puff to surrender. He answered with gunfire. Agents posted behind parked cars returned the fire and Puff collapsed to the sidewalk.

He was taken to a hospital for treatment, then to the prison ward at Bellevue. Special Agent Brock was treated by a doctor who appeared on the scene, then rushed to a hospital where he was pronounced dead shortly after arrival.

Newspapers in many places reported the death of the FBI agent. Some, through a release from INS, quoted the "lone eyewitness" to the murder, who was actually hiding in his office when he heard the gunshots.

The July 26 article, credited to Louis Baker, manager of the Congress Hotel in New York, reported the following:

> I took Agent Brock down the lobby corridor when we got a phone call saying Puff and his friends were going to check out. While the other G-men stayed in the office or posted themselves in the street, Brock took up a station near the partly open glazed glass door which seperates the elevators from the stair exits.
>
> Brock crouched down by the door, apparently expecting that Puff would come down in the elevator and he could surprise him when the door slid open.

The Prodigal Puff

I started to walk back to the hotel office when suddenly I heard a shot –maybe two—from the stair exit. As I ran –scared to death—to the office, I heard Brock cry out in pain, "Help, I'm hurt."

I rushed into the office and shouted to the room clerk to duck down. Before the words were out of my mouth the six or seven FBI men in the office tore out the door and chased Puff into the street.

I could hear people screaming and shouting in the street. Then there was a flurry of shots as the FBI men closed in on Puff. I heard later he had been shot in the left leg and had been taken into custody.

When Puff and another man and two women registered last Sunday I had no idea they were anything but persons who were going to stay in New York for a long visit.

Puff – who registered as J. Burn—the other man, Mr. Hansen, and the two women had three elevator loads of baggage among them. I gave them two rooms, one on the ninth floor, one on the sixth.

Yesterday, the two women – both of them pretty nice looking – called the desk for a taxi.

They had a lot of luggage when they got in the cab and drove away. Then a couple of hours later the two men also went out in a cab.

At 6:30 last night, Puff (Burn) and Mrs. Hansen came back, asked that their bill be prepared, and went up to their rooms. They went out again without paying the bill, or taking their bags.

The FBI brought some pictures over last night

and asked me if the guy on the wanted poster was the man registered as Burn. I said, I couldn't tell. Then they showed me another picture of "Burn" and "Mrs. Burn" in a night club. I said I thought I recognized them. The G-men stayed in the hotel all night, some of them in the room on the main floor. At 12:30 p. m. today both women came back to the hotel. Mrs. Hansen then took some bags and went out again.

An FBI radio car followed her to another hotel, and then back to the Congress. She went back upstairs.

A few minutes later Burn came in and went up to his ninth floor room. The agents were in my office when Burn called and said he was checking out and wanted his bill. That's when I took Agent Bock down the corridor to the door, where he waited for Puff and was shot to death.

The United States Southern District Court of New York found Gerhard guilty of murder on May 15, 1953. He was sentenced to death in the electric chair. For more than a year, the attorney appointed for Gerhard sought to appeal Gerhard's conviction. A plea was made to President Dwight D. Eisenhower to grant clemency in the case, but the justice department announced in early 1954 that the clemency request had been denied. His execution had been set for June 21, 1954, but the date had been stayed pending the outcome of a possible appeal and the clemency request. A new date of August 12, 1954, was set.

The Prodigal Puff

Gerhard sent a hand-written letter to Heinz just weeks before the scheduled date for his execution. Dated July 19, 1954, and displaying excellent handwriting, it read:

Dear Heinz:

    Have received your letter. Thanks loads. Sorry not to have answered sooner, but I delayed purposely until a decision was handed down by the United States Supreme Court Judge Black pending a further stays so my three attorneys could continue with the notice of motion brief in support of same under U. S. Code 28, #2255, which is foreign to you. But my stay was denied and there is no further relief open to me. My execution date has been set for this July 28th. My only remaining remedy is executive clemency to the President of our Country. There are many things I would like to ask you and again as many, I'd enjoy telling. As for visiting me, Heinz, you know you would be welcome, but I don't think you should waste the money it would take traveling all that distance. Should you decide in favor of it, the only one allowed in without special permission or Court Order would be you and Dad, any other member would not be allowed at the spur of the moment. Thursdays is legal execution date + no visiting, being a federal prisoner, I leave Wednesday 11 p. m. I might mention that the only one allowed visits on the day of execution is the party involved. Heinz, you know I'll never think nothing but the best of you and Dad or any member of our family. I'm sure glad to hear Dad is O. K. How do you like your job? As a cop, do they kid brother a copper? Only kidding. Be a good one, Heinz. Say hello to Caroline and be good to her. I also experienced marriage and learned for the first time in my life to be completely, happily in love with my wife Annie Laurie, one of the most beautiful girls I've ever seen. Although she is only 19 years of age, she has suffered very severely in becoming my wife and is still at the present detained in a girls reformatory not far from here. But alas, she loves me and writes to me constantly as I do to her. Also, my Mother-in Law, thinks a lot of me and writes regularly. Would I have met her much sooner, I know I would not be here today. Perhaps that sounds weak, but you know I'm not. Give Dad my regards and tell him I wish him the best of health and a long happy life. The same to Ida and Ma. Say goodbye to Caroline's Mom + Dad, real nice people. That about winds up all I have to say in this letter. I will tell you Good bye and wish you from the bottom of my heart all the happiness in the world and a long life to you and your little family.

With all sincerity
Your Brother
Gerhard A. Puff

The execution did take place on August 12, as scheduled, and it was performed by the newly-hired executioner at Sing Sing who also turned out to be Sing Sing's last executioner. In 2005, an article titled "The Last Executioner," by Jennifer Gonnerman, appeared in the New York *Village Voice*. It told the story of a deputy sheriff and trained electrician who was hired as executioner at Sing Sing. He held this position until 1963, when the last execution at Sing Sing took place.

The Prodigal Puff

Photo from Sing Sing Prison

The article mentions that Gerhard Puff was "one of the first people [he] was hired to execute."

Heinz and Caroline struggled with the question of making the trip to New York to see Gerhard one last time. There was the cost concern, but that was clearly secondary. They questioned whether a visit would make things worse or better, particularly if his father went along. Heinz and his father, Arthur, had visited Gerhard a number of times when he was incarcerated in Wisconsin. On those visits, they would plead with Gerhard to change his ways. Gerhard always seemed oblivious to their pleas. It was as if he couldn't understand why they were so concerned, any more than they could understand why he was so oblivious. As the time of Gerhard's execution drew closer, there were other questions for Heinz. Would the very last memory of Gerhard be the one emblazoned in his and his father's minds for all time? Could they do anything to help Gerhard? Could they assure him of their love? He already knew that, though he may not have fully realized their utter distain for what he had done. Could it have any negative impact upon his job or could he become the focus of stories about Gerhard and his sentence? In the final analysis, Heinz decided not to make the trip, though he has, at times, questioned that decision. While communication from Gerhard to Heinz strongly suggested that Heinz not come for a visit before his execution, this was not the motivating factor. Heinz knew that Gerhard had been characterized publicly as a "lonely" inmate, but he was simply unsure of how a visit would help.

For years, Heinz chose not to talk about his brother or his brother's final demise. It was too painful—a story too difficult to share. Heinz and Caroline knew, even as Gerhard's execution approached, that it would never be completely "over." Heinz had chosen a path in life that Gerhard, apparently, never would have chosen, for whatever the reasons may have been. And Gerhard had chosen a path in life that Heinz would never have chosen, even considered, or could ever comprehend.

"I was the one authorized legally to carry a gun," says Heinz. "He was not. Fortunately, as a police officer, I never had to use mine to kill another person. He used a weapon, not to help keep the peace, but to break the peace. I felt nothing but respect for agencies

The Prodigal Puff

of law enforcement. He had little respect for them and did everything to keep his distance from them. In the final analysis, it was the weapon that made such a big difference. Like many things, a tool can be used for good or evil. I'd like to think mine was always used for good ... and wish his had never been used at all."

Milwaukee newspapers and others around the country reported on the execution with a story filed by Associated Press. The headline was "Murderer of FBI Agent Dies in Sing Sing - Whitefish Bay Man Electrocuted for 1952 Gun Battle":

> Bank robber Gerhard A. Puff – once one of the FBI's "10 most wanted" criminals – died in the electric chair at Sing Sing prison Thursday night for the murder of an FBI agent. New York state carried out the execution for the federal government.
>
> The Rev. Fred D. Kuether, protestant federal prison chaplain, accompanied Puff, whose family lives at Whitefish Bay, Wis. , as he walked into the death chamber with a smile and looked around.
>
> Puff then looked at United States Marshal Thomas J. Lunney and said "Goodbye, Marshal," before sitting down in the chair.
>
> Puff, 40, was executed for the shooting of FBI agent Joseph J. Brock, 42, in a gun battle as FBI men closed in on him and several companions in the Congress Hotel in New York City July 26, 1952.
>
> The agents wanted Puff for the robbery of a Prairie Village, Kan. , bank. The jury in United States District

PUFF

Court in New York city convicted Puff of the murder.

Puff didn't have a visitor during nearly 15 months in the death house. His wife, Annie Laurie Puff, 19, was in jail and relatives shunned him as fruitless appeals to save him from the death chair were made by his attorneys.

A sawed-off shotgun was found in the wife's luggage at the time of Puff's capture. She is serving two years in a state correctional institution at Bedford Hills.

Sing Sing Warden Wilfred L Denno refused to let the wife visit Puff because their marriage was bigamous. Puff was not divorced from his first wife. The two prisoners, however, exchanged letters. President Eisenhower denied Puff clemency last week.

Puff's father, Arthur, and a brother, Heinz, live in Whitefish Bay.

Heinz has never stopped being just a little bit curious about the actual circumstances surrounding the capture of Gerhard and the shooting of the agent. There was only one witness, and he was not close to the scene of the murder. Since the hotel was heavily stacked-out with a full contingent of FBI agents, it is not inconceivable that the gunfire that killed Agent Joseph J. Brock could have been "friendly fire" from another FBI agent. To Heinz's knowledge, no ballistic report on the bullet or bullets that killed the agent was ever made public. Heinz's curiosity about what happened that day in the New York hotel has never been satisfied. Maybe it's just a lingering doubt, born of his many years as a police officer. The unfortunate reality, as Heinz is quick to affirm, was that Gerhard put himself in that position. Choosing criminal activity, and at some point choosing to arm himself with a gun, simply left him in the position of being susceptible to precisely what happened.

Heinz is at a loss, too, about the way in which Gerhard's execution was expedited. Heinz wonders why other inmates spent years on death row. Gerhard's stay was quite a bit shorter. Was it because the crime involved an FBI agent? Heinz will never know for sure, but the question lingers in his mind.

Of course, Heinz grieved for the family of Agent Brock. No matter what the precise circumstance, a fellow law enforcement person had lost his life.

V

ENOUGH!

The day did come when Heinz thought it might be time to hang up the spurs. He was still young and healthy, and he loved northern Wisconsin. Fishing and spending more time with Caroline might be nice.

Heinz knew he had been blessed. He had faced guns and knives, and clubs, and riots and had been in a variety of situations where his life could have ended. Maybe leaving in one piece was not a bad idea. Having met the requirement of 25 years of service, at the age of 52, Heinz called it quits. It disappointed his captain, who tried to talk Heinz out of retirement, saying "Heinz, you are one of the best I ever had." But after discussing it with Caroline, he made the decision. They would move to the area of God's creation they loved, not far from where they had honeymooned.

There was one concern, however: Caroline's parents, who were living close to Heinz and Caroline. One night during a visit to the in-laws' apartment, Heinz announced that he and Caroline would be moving north, and asked if they would like to come along. "You could live with us," offered Heinz. Heinz was close to his in-laws. They had always been good to him. Now they were getting up in years and experiencing some health problems, and Heinz just couldn't see being five or six hours separated from them. What if they really needed help? It would be difficult.

When Heinz and Caroline got in the car to head home that evening, Caroline, in a voice that commanded attention, said "Heinz, are you nuts? We raised our children, we have a chance to retire . . . to live an easier life . . . and you invite my *parents* to come along? What are you thinking?"

Well, Caroline knew that Heinz not only liked his in-laws, but he was quite concerned about them, as well. Of course, she understood. Separation from them and constant worry about them in Milwaukee would not have made for an easy life, either. So the plan was set.

The Minocqua area was a natural for Heinz and Caroline. Heinz's father had acquired some land on Little Spider Lake, just north of town, while Heinz was serving in the military. When Heinz returned from service, he helped his father complete the building of a cabin on the land. Heinz had fallen in love with this part of God's creation as a young man. In fact, Heinz and Caroline had spent their honeymoon at a small resort just several miles from his father's cabin.

The town of Minocqua, whose name is believed to be Chippewa, is situated in a vast area of lakes and forests. Its small population of 5,000 more than doubles in summer with all of the recreational visitors and vacation home-owners who spend most of the colder months elsewhere. Even with a small population, the Minocqua area today boasts many fine retail establishments, restaurants and ample medical facilities. It has been an excellent home for the Puffs, who have enjoyed hunting, fishing, summer and winter sports and four-season beauty.

True to his word, Heinz moved Caroline's parents to the new home they built on Little Spider Lake in the mid-1970s. Caroline, who first called Heinz "nuts" for offering to invite her parents to live with them, was happy with the arrangement. Her parents were residents in their home until her father died at the age of 90 and her mother died shortly thereafter at the age of 86.

For the most part, Heinz was able to leave behind his time as a police officer, as he had his army experiences. The new surroundings and the distance from Milwaukee helped create the sense of starting over. He lost touch with most of those with whom he had worked on the force. He did stay in touch with several, including Bob Miotke, the person he called his "favorite sergeant." Having chosen to retire, it was time to begin another new phase of his life, and he did so with great enthusiasm and anticipation.

Not being ones to simply sit around and spend all of their time fishing (as much as they enjoyed fishing), Heinz and Carol soon found ways to occupy at least part of their time. Heinz got a job as a school bus driver. His daily route covered a rather wide area in north central Wisconsin. He was up at 4:00 in the morning – earlier on snowy winter days – and would complete his run by 8:00 in the morning. In the afternoon, the route would be traversed in reverse.

"I actually enjoyed the job," Heinz admitted. "So many of the drivers complained about the kids and the crazy things they would say and do on the bus. I liked the youngsters and had very little trouble with them. It proved something I have tried to practice in my life: If you show concern and respect for others, you will likely get much of the same in return. It works with young people, too. I demanded proper behavior, but there's a way to do that without being considered 'mean.' We actually had a good time together on the bus. And for some of the kids, because of the length of the drive, I was probably together with them more than they were with their parents. When I finally decided to stop driving the bus, I found myself missing the kids."

Caroline didn't sit on her hands, either. She cared

Enough!

for her parents while they were still alive, and also opened a small resale shop in Woodruff, The Fair Exchange, that she operated for more than 18 years. It provided a little income, but more than that, it gave her a chance to interact with people. Caroline was always a people person, loved by all those who came to know her. Of course, she also continued to love fishing.

Heinz and Caroline had friends in the northwoods whom they saw often. They enjoyed get-togethers, card games, a drink or two, swimming in the lake, gatherings around bonfires, and snowmobiling in the winter. In fact, they were among the first to have the new-fangled contraptions known as snowmobiles. Their place on the lake is just a few hundred feet from what became a snowmobile trail. Many trails in northern Wisconsin were formed on abandoned railroad grades. In the depth of winter, snowmobiling on Little Spider Lake and other area lakes was commonplace. They loved the sport and didn't give it up until they were approaching the age of 80.

Their children, Carol and Gary, appreciated many of the things their parents did. Gary was a fisherman and a hunter who loved the outdoors. Carol, who lives in England with her husband and children, still made her way to Little Spider Lake several times a year. She enjoys fishing, too, and helped in her mother's shop whenever she was visiting.

No retirement is absolutely ideal. But Heinz and Caroline's has been above average. What has marked their time together is a closeness to one another and to their family. To this day, a normal routine for them is a game of cards before dinner. It used to be penny-ante, but in recent years it has become dime-ante. And they are as competitive as ever.

Oh, the fishing continues, too. Normally they take enough fish out of Little Spider Lake to fill a nice portion of their freezer so that they can enjoy them all winter long.

Heinz and Caroline have a wonderful appreciation for simple things. Heinz enjoys reading and has read more books than there are in some small libraries. He has even been known to write some poetry. He likes to cook, and he especially likes cooking some of Caroline's favorite meals for her. For many years he was a wine-maker. Some claim his cranberry wine was among the finest.

Caroline still loves to dance. The polka is not really the type of music she once pursued professionally, but she moves well with it, nonetheless. And speaking of opera—the type of music she once did pursue—she has records (yes, records, and some CDs, as well) that get a lot of use in the house they built on Little Spider.

Heinz and Caroline are gifted people. They have accomplished quite a lot. But they have never expected any special favors as a result.

Heinz seldom mentions that he is a World War II veteran. Like many veterans of the World War II era, Heinz seems reluctant to recall the many things war brought into his consciousness. Nor is he inclined to make a big deal of the fact that he is a retired police officer. One night, when returning home from a dance in the area, Heinz was pulled over by a patrolling police officer for going slightly above the speed limit. The friends in the back seat said, "Be sure you tell him you are a retired police officer." But Heinz, of course, chose not to do so. The officer gave Heinz a warning, not a ticket. But it wasn't because Heinz tried to take advantage of his former position. As Heinz would say, "If I'm wrong, I'm wrong and I deserve the same consequences as anyone else."

POSTSCRIPT

Stories of Heinz and Caroline will be told for many years to come. Their endurance, excellent humor, and devotion to one another are qualities everyone should emulate.

Anyone who knows them will talk about the banter that takes place between them. Listening to it, some might conclude that they really don't like each other. Quite to the contrary, it is a classic example of "picking on someone you love." They probably could have gone on the road for many years as a comedy act.

They both love to talk. Caroline says that Heinz gets the most air time. Heinz disagrees and claims it's difficult to get a word in. He says, "Modern medical science is wonderful, but they still haven't figured out how to treat Caroline's mouth." Despite that difference of opinion, they are always anxious to listen to what others have to say. "Tell me about . . ." or "How is . . . ?" or "So what ever happened with . . . ?" are among the first exchanges with visiting friends.

PUFF

One of the stories that survives concerns a member of the family that owns the cottage next door to Heinz and Caroline. At this particular time, no family member was at the cottage. A young man of the family, who didn't spend much time at the lake, showed up in the very early morning hours to spend a few days. When he arrived, he realized he had not remembered a key to get into the cottage. So he went next door to the Puffs. As he tells it, he knocked on the door. He then waited a bit and knocked again. A light came on in the Puff house. The door opened slowly to reveal Heinz, stark naked, with a shotgun in his hands. "Come on in," said Heinz. "Want to sit down?" All the while the young "intruder" was wondering where to look and what to say. "Never seen a naked man?" Heinz asked. "I have not slept in pajamas since my time in New Guinea and the Philippines. Couldn't stand 'em then. Too hot, and I was always sweaty. And when I got home, I just couldn't stand the idea of ever wearing pajamas again. So, the next time you forget your keys at this time of the night, just know that I will appear again in this way ... *and* with the shotgun."

Heinz, and Caroline just seemed always to make life brighter for those around them. But, as you can tell from what is recorded in this book, life for them was not always easy.

The most tragic event of their lives occurred in

Postscript

Heinz's son, Gary Puff, in the Army.

2008. Their son, Gary, just 59 years old, died very suddenly of a heart attack.

Gary had followed in his father's footsteps. He, too, served in the military, including two tours in Viet Nam. And again, like his father, he chose a career in law enforcement. Prior to becoming a police officer, he served on an ambulance crew, during which time he enrolled in a "police science" course of studies. Eventually, he was hired by the Shorewood, Wisconsin, police department. Gary was a police officer for 20 years and when given the chance to retire, he consulted his father. "You're still alive," said his father. "Don't push it. If you have a chance to retire, do so!"

Gary was always close to his parents. He and his

wife, Nancy (also a police officer) spent a lot of time with Heinz and Caroline at the lake. They helped with work around the house, helped with the boats (even buying Heinz and Caroline a brand new fishing boat several years before Gary died) and enjoyed fishing as much as Heinz and Caroline did. Gary was a wonderful son who even inherited a bit of his father's sometimes off-beat sense of humor.

One story Heinz tells is of the time Gary and some fellow officers decided to play a prank on a superior officer they felt "deserved a taste of humility." The superior officer was a pipe-smoker. And when the opportunity presented itself, behind the superior's back, they loaded his pipe with marijuana they had seized in the course of their work. You can imagine how humiliating it was for the pipe-smoker to be filling the police station with the aroma of burning marijuana.

Carol Puff at her confirmation.

Perhaps as a last and final touch of humor, Gary's cremated ashes were placed prominently at his funeral in a fishing tackle box. He had told his wife that when the time came, that was the most appropriate place for his ashes.

Heinz and Caroline think of Gary "all the time." There are photos of Gary all over their house.

Postscript

Occasionally, you can find Caroline talking to the pictures as if she was talking with her son across the table. Despite having suffered the most horrible loss for any parent, Heinz says "we were so blessed with Gary. What a great son. I don't know what we did to deserve a son like him, but we were certainly grateful to God to have him." And he says the same thing about Gary's sister, Carol, who is still very much a part of his and Caroline's life.

Carol was the firstborn Puff child. Like Gary, she, too, inherited some of the endearing characteristics of her parents. Having grown up in Milwaukee, she attended the University of Wisconsin, Milwaukee, in a course designed to prepare legal assistants. Following her studies, she and a girl friend were determined to find a way to travel. Both wanted to see Europe. It was truly a long shot, but they both sent resumés to law firms in England before boarding the Queen Elizabeth II for a trip to that destination. The effort was rewarded. Carol got a job with a large law firm in London. Before too long, she met a manufacturer's rep by the name of Steve Payne. After a period of time, Steve and Carol made the trip to the states to share with Heinz and Caroline their plans to marry. In a most respectful way, Steve approached Heinz asking for Carol's hand.

In a manner typical of Heinz's sense of humor

he responded, "No . . . I'd suggest you take the whole body." Heinz and Caroline were not fond of the idea of Carol living permanently in England, but they were happy for her and supportive of her desire to make a home in England with Steve.

Despite the distance separating them, Carol frequently travels to spend time with her parents. Her children and grandchildren come occasionally, too. In earlier days, Heinz and Caroline would travel to England and always enjoyed their time in that part of the world.

Despite the number of events in their lives that were anything but pleasant, their attitude remains positive and their love for one another remains secure—even though, Heinz says, "It's been 'tough' living for so many years with a crazy Hungarian." In 2011, the always-on-the-go Caroline broke a leg. For the first time in her life, she was really confined and unable to get around. Nevertheless, she cheered up the people who cared for her in the hospital and the rehabilitation center. Heinz, himself a very good cook, had to do it with more regularity. While Caroline was confined, Heinz quipped, "I'm putting on weight now that I'm getting some decent home cooking."

When one of their friends learned that Caroline had to return temporarily to the hospital after having been released, he asked Heinz what the problem

Postscript

was. Heinz's response? "They think she might be pregnant."

If it is true that "you pick on the ones you love," then the love Heinz and Caroline have for each other has remained strong for many, many years.

They often talk of how blessed they have been. And they credit God for His goodness to them. They are proud of their children and are grateful for the love shown to them by their children. They miss Gary and think of him often, and always relish the time they are able to spend with their daughter, Carol.

As for his brother, a poem written by Robert Frost around the time Heinz was born may capture the quandary. "Two roads diverged . . ." wrote Frost. Frost concludes the poem by stating that the "one less traveled by . . . made all the difference." One can speculate on what the difference was. It could be said that both Heinz and Gerhard took roads less traveled. Heinz chose first to be a soldier, then chose a profession not many choose. All along the way, he chose positive values and a life of integrity. Gerhard chose a destructive lifestyle that few, but far too many, choose. For both, the choices made all the difference. The brothers took truly divergent roads. Heinz would always wish that Gerhard had taken a road similar to the one he chose.

"It's been quite a ride," says Heinz. And that may

be due, in part, to a simple way of looking at life. As Heinz says, "I've lived on this lake for many years. We have a fine view of the sun setting over the lake. Sometimes it is beautiful. Sometimes the sun itself is obscured by storm clouds or lost in a blinding blizzard. Still, in all the years we have lived here, not once has the sun failed to rise the next morning." Obvious, you might say; but what a powerful testimony to faith, to never giving up, to focusing on the bigger picture, and to a confidence in the future that will one day transcend Little Spider Lake.

Sunrise over Little Spider Lake

Heinz Puff (far right) with wife Caroline, daughter Carol, and author Paul Devantier. Photo taken at Marty's Place North Restaurant on Little Spider Lake in Arbor Vitae, Wisconsin, in March 2011.